Recent Advances

in

CRISIS INTERVENTION

edited by

Dr. N. RAO PUNUKOLLU

associate editor
JULIE JACKSON

assistant editors
DAVID SHARP
and
DAVID STORR

 INTERNATIONAL INSTITUTE OF CRISIS
INTERVENTION AND COMMUNITY PSYCHIATRY
PUBLICATIONS
Huddersfield

List of Contributors

Howard J. Parad, MSW, DSW, LCSW
Professor Emeritus, University of Southern California, Los Angeles, U.S.A.

Libbie G. Parad, MSW, DSW, LCSW
Formerly Senior Administrator, Orange County Division of Children and Youth Services, Santa Ana, U.S.A.

Dr. N. Rao Punukollu, MBBS, DPM, MRCPsych
Consultant Psychiatrist, St. Luke's Hospital, Huddersfield.

Dr. Donald G. Langsley, MD
Executive Vice-President of American Board of Medical Specialities, Illinois, U.S.A.

Dr. John Hoult
Senior Psychiatrist, Glebe Community Care Centre, New South Wales, Australia.

Dr. L. Ratna, MBBS, DPM, MRCPsych.
Consultant Psychiatrist, Barnet General Hospital, Hertfordshire, U.K.

Dr. R. Denis Scott, MB, BCh., MRCP, FRCPsych.
Consultant Psychiatrist, Muswell Hill, London, U.K.

Dr. J. A. Jenner, MD, PhD
Senior Lecturer, University of Gronningen, The Netherlands.

Dr. J. Stelzer, MD
Psychiatrist, Manitoba, Canada.

Dr. Douglas A. Puryear, MD
Director, Psychiatric Emergency Services, Parkland Memorial Hospital, Dallas, U.S.A.

Dr. Yoshihiro Ishikawa, DMPsych., DPMH
Chief Researcher (Dept. of Psychopathology) Research Institute of Tokyo, Tokyo, Japan.

Prof. Berthold P.R. Gersons, MD
Professor of Ambulatory Social Psychiatry, Academic Hospital, Utrecht, The Netherlands.

(cont.)

Prof. Rachel M. Rosser, MA, MB, BChir., PhD, FRCP, FRCPsych.
  Head of Dept. of Psychiatry, University College and Middlesex School
  of Medicine, London, U.K.

Dr. Gary M. Jackson, MBB.Ch., MRCPsych.
  Dept. of Psychiatry, University College and Middlesex School of
  Medicine, London (U.K.)

Dr. Joseph J. Zealberg, MD
  Director, Emergency Psychiatric Services, South Carolina, U.S.A.

Dr. Helle Aggernæs, MD
  Frederiksberg Hospital, Copenhagen, Denmark.

Dr. S. Schepelern, MD
  Frederiksberg Hospital, Copenhagen, Denmark.

Michael Ash
  Nurse Co-ordinator, Psychiatric Emergency Team, Health Department
  of Western Australia.

Ms. Helen Cleak
  Senior Tutor, La Trobe University, Bundoora, Australia.

Contents

Preface
N. Rao Punukollu

(cont.)

Preface

This book is based on papers presented to the First International Conference on "Crisis Intervention Approach in Mental Health", held in London during June, 1990.

The conference was attended by speakers and delegates from 34 countries; the following chapters reflect the work carried out world-wide relating to Crisis theory, practice and research, and brought together at that conference.

The National Institute of Crisis Intervention Therapy and Research was established during 1988 to organise educational programmes on social and community aspects of mental health, and to disseminate information about recent developments in Crisis Intervention. This volume is published as part of those aims; a further collection will be published as Volume 2.

We would like to extend our thanks to the authors of these diverse papers for their contributions, and to friends and colleagues working in Crisis Intervention teams across the world for their support.

Crisis Intervention: Yesterday, Today and Tomorrow *

Howard J. Parad and Libbie G. Parad

Crisis intervention is no longer the experimental fad many considered it to be 30 years ago when the authors, among others, helped introduce the crisis approach. Mental health professionals and other human services personnel are increasingly attracted to brief crisis intervention as an effective method of delivering readily accessible and rapid services to many people experiencing acute situational and interpersonal stress, life-cycle and other transitional changes, and natural and man-made disasters. These services are offered by various social work agencies, such as family counselling, neighbourhood centres, public social service, and child welfare agencies, as well as in many multidisciplinary settings, such as community mental health centres, emergency walk-in clinics, suicide prevention and hotline services, hospitals, and disaster-aid centres.

In this chapter we shall address, among others, the following questions:

1. What is a crisis and what is crisis intervention?
2. What are the differences and similarities between crisis intervention and brief therapy?
3. Why is crisis intervention important in the field of human services?
4. What is the historical background of crisis intervention?
5. What are some of the practice applications of the crisis approach?
6. What can we predict about the future of crisis intervention?

What is a crisis?

Simply put, a crisis is an upset in a steady state, a turning point leading to better or worse, a disruption or breakdown in a person's or family's normal and usual pattern of functioning. The upset, or disequilibrium, is usually acute in the sense that it is of recent origin. However, when working with a crisis-prone person, a "crisis junkie", acute crises may erupt in a chronic situation (Kagan & Schlosberg, 1989). The pain and discomfort of a crisis may be assessed both subjectively, as perceived by the victim, or "objectively" by an observer. The severity of a crisis may be rated along a continuum from mild to moderate to severe.

How does crisis differ from a problem or an emergency? Some mental health professionals consider an emergency situation to exist only when a person is thought to be dangerous to self or others or is gravely disabled - a broad term that refers to a person's inability to feed, clothe, or otherwise to care for him- or herself. Many professionals, dissatisfied with the imprecision of most formal definitions of crisis, take the practical view that

---

* Adapted from: Howard J. Parad & Libbie G. Parad (eds.) (1990) *Crisis Intervention Book 2: The Practitioner's Sourcebook for Brief Therapy* Milwaukee, Wi.:Family Service America.

if clients believe they must be seen immediately, they are experiencing an emergency situation; if they can wait twenty-four to seventy-two hours, they are in a crisis; and if they can wait for a longer period, they may merely be experiencing a problem..

Regardless of what definition of crisis is used, professionals generally agree that crisis intervention focuses on a range of phenomena that affect the biopsychosocial functioning of an individual, family, or group, creating a state of disequilibrium. These phenomena include stresses relating to disordered communication patterns, disrupted networks of role relationships, and dissonant values. The causes of these dysfunctional phenomena are as varied as the families and individuals who experience them and as complicated as the neighbourhoods and larger social systems in which these individuals, families, and groups live.

In a general sense, crisis intervention is a process for actively influencing psychosocial functioning during a period of disequilibrium in order to alleviate the immediate impact of disruptive stressful events and to help mobilise the manifest and latent psychological capabilities and social resources of persons directly affected by the crisis (and often the key persons in the social environment) for coping adaptively with the effects of stress. More specifically, the crisis clinician's interventive efforts have two principal aims: (a) to cushion the stressful event by immediate or emergency emotional and environmental first aid and (b) to strengthen the person in his or her coping and integrative struggles through immediate therapeutic clarification and guidance during the crisis period.

Concept of crisis

Crisis is a useful conceptual device for understanding the behaviour of individuals and families under stress. However, there has been some confusion regarding terminology. For example, it is difficult to objectively differentiate "stress" - the specific event that may precipitate a crisis - from "strain" - the response to that event. Stress and crisis are often used interchangeably, thus robbing the term "crisis" of precise meaning. Although all people face stress as part of the human condition, not all stressful experiences produce crisis situations.

References to crisis intervention as a theory are another source of confusion. The constructs and techniques of the crisis approach - like virtually all psychotherapeutic modalities - lack the formal attributes of systematically validated scientific theory (Auerbach & Stolberg, 1986). However, a growing body of clinical research concerning stress-response phenomena (Horowitz & Kaltreider, 1980; Horowitz, 1986) provides a promising pathway toward developing a science of crisis intervention. Our sourcebook (Parad & Parad, 1990) offers practice applications of Horowitz's stress-response research.

Crisis sequence

Because the stress-crisis sequence involves a complex set of biopsychosocial forces, we view crisis as a configuration involving (1) a specific and identifiable *stressful precipitating event,* (2) the *perception* of the event as meaningful and threatening, (3) the disorganisation or disequilibrium *response* resulting from the stressful event, and (4) the coping and interventive tasks involved in *resolution,* which may be adaptive or maladaptive. The term "configuration" is used to convey the idea that the phases of the crisis sequence are interlocking. For purposes of analysis, however, it is necessary to separate the components of the configuration. A crisis intervention approach pays attention to the elements of this configuration as well as to the prompt accessibility of treatment, which should be as close as possible to the impact of the stress and crisis response. In essence, then, the crisis state reflects the perception of and response to an internal or external stress that is experienced by the individual or individuals involved as a threat to vital goals such as life, security, and affectional ties. Our definition of the crisis configuration (see Figure 1) is adapted from Hill's (1965) classic formulation of the intervening variables that "transform a stressor event into a crisis" (p36). Hill's conceptual framework outlines the following ABCX formula, which is applicable to individuals as well as to families:

FIGURE 1
*The Crisis Intervention "roller coaster" ***

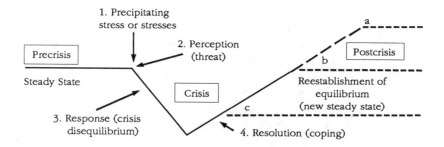

1. Precipitating stress (triggering event or events)
2. Perception (threatening to life goals, affectional ties, security)
3. Response (crisis state, with signs of disequilibrium)
4. Resolution (adaptive or maladaptive coping with crisis tasks)
   a. New postcrisis equilibrium is better than the precrisis steady state.
   b. Postcrisis equilibrium is about the same as precrisis state.
   c. New postcrisis equilibrium is less satisfactory than the
      precrisis state.

Adapted from Hill, R. (1965) Generic Features of Families under Stress. In H.J. Parad (Ed.) *Crisis Intervention: Selected Readings* (p.32-52). New York: Family Service Association of America. Used with permission.

"A (the stressor event) interacting with B (the family's crisis-meeting resources) —> interacting with C (the definition the family makes of the event) —> produces X (the crisis)" (p36).

Studying families in crisis, McCubbin and Patterson (1983) and Van Hook (1987) expanded Hill's formula by advancing a "double ABCX model," which focuses over time on the dynamic interactions among participants in the crisis drama and the effects of these interactions on crisis outcome. For example, in her study of distressed farm families, Van Hook points out that during an economic crisis a farmer's wife may seek outside employment. This coping effort leads to an increase in family income, which is adaptive for the family. The wife's employment, however, may create a new stress for the husband if she is less emotionally available to him than she was during the precrisis steady state. The husband may then perceive the wife's new status as threatening to their relationship. Thus a new crisis may be induced as part of the trade-off cost for crisis resolution. Basic to this expanded model of interactional crisis phenomena is the understanding that perceptions of and responses to stress reflect the participants' sense of internal as well as external reality and therefore have reciprocal, reverberating effects within the circularity of the family system (Van Hook, 1987). The interconnected assumptions (Parad, 1977), commonly used to explain the phenomena of the crisis sequence, have been discussed in detail by Lindemann (1956) and Caplan (1964) - the two main formulators of the crisis approach.

Timing and time limits

During the active state of crisis, the person experiences a turning point. Sooner or later, but generally within four to six weeks according to Lindemann and Caplan, things get better or worse because nature abhors a vacuum. Thus a state of crisis is by its very nature time-limited. A minimum of therapeutic intervention during the brief crisis period can often produce a maximum therapeutic effect through the use of supportive social resources and focused treatment techniques. Hence, crisis intervention services are usually short-term.

Whereas crisis intervention services are usually brief, not all brief therapy is to be equated with crisis intervention. Crisis intervention may involve a specific or approximate number of interviews or weeks of treatment as part of the treatment arrangement. Several rationales have been offered for the desirability of time limits in therapy. One commonly advanced argument is that time limits may increase the client's *and* the worker's motivation.

The seemingly simple question of how brief is brief treatment is actually very complex. Some professionals consider brief treatment to consist of a single session; others think it should involve approximately six sessions; still others define brief therapy as extending up to twenty or even forty or more interviews (Budman & Gurman, 1988). A nationwide study of crisis-oriented treatment in family counselling agencies and children's psychiatric services demonstrated that from 80% to 90% of all planned short-term cases were seen for up to twelve interviews over a period of up to 3 months (Parad & Parad, 1968). A *planned* short-term treatment (PSTT) approach involves the designation of a predetermined specific number of interviews or weeks of treatment within the first or second session with the client, family or group.

Time and timing are important in crisis counselling. Practice-derived wisdom suggests that access to help should be available early and that help is best timed at the onset of a crisis experience. However, issues such as how many contacts there should be, how they should be spaced, and for what duration for each individual, family, or other small group are less settled. Mental health practice tends to be flexible and is often based on matters of expediency as well as on the style and temperament of practitioners. There seems to be no magic in the six-week pattern of crisis intervention first suggested by Caplan, although in a nationwide study six was the modal number of interviews used in PSTT crisis-oriented programmes (Parad & Parad, 1968). Practice, of course, varies greatly, from marathon groups to once-a-week sessions for six to twelve or more weeks. Empirically derived findings concerning the optimal number, frequency, and spacing of treatment contacts would be useful to those interested in both crisis intervention and brief therapy.

The paradigm presented in Table 1 attempts to clarify the use of the crisis approach and the structured use of time in mental health practice. As indicated in this paradigm, the following are four logical service categories with respect to the dimensions of crisis and time:

TABLE 1
*Use of the crisis approach and the time dimension in
mental health practice*

PSTT	Non-PSTT
Crisis oriented	
1.	2.
Early accessibility at time of request for help (within 24 - 72 hours of the "cry for help")	Early accessibility at time of request for help (within 24 - 72 hours of the "cry for help")
Use of PSTT limits (specific number or approximate range of interviews or weeks - determined at intake - to be utilised during crisis response and resolution phases)	Open-ended orientation toward time dimension; duration of contact may be informally brief (no time contract made during intake phase, that is, first or second interviews; or contact may be "long-term":
Use of task-centred techniques	crisis intervention may be regarded
Focused attention to crisis configuration (precipitating event, perception of threat, response, and resolution)	primarily as point of entry into an extended treatment service.
	Some attention to elements of crisis configuration.
(+ +)	(+ -)

PSTT	Non-PSTT
Noncrisis oriented	
3.	4.
May be short or long waiting period	May be short or long waiting period
Use of PSTT limits: contract for specific	Open-ended orientation toward time
predetermined number of interviews,	dimension; no use of PSTT limits
determined at intake	No special attention to crisis
Use of task-centred or other goal-oriented	configuration
techniques	May be oriented to specific or diffuse goals
No special attention to crisis configuration	
(- +)	(- -)

1. PSTT crisis-oriented services: A great deal of crisis intervention work falls within this cell.
2. Non-PSTT crisis-oriented services: The crisis may afford entry to open-ended, long-term therapy.
3. PSTT non crisis-oriented services: Many forms of brief therapy are offered in human service programmes (see Budman, 1981; Budman & Gurman, 1988).
4. Services that are neither PSTT nor crisis-oriented, that is, most traditional psychodynamic and other open-ended therapies.

This paradigm clarifies a point all too frequently confused by many practitioners - namely, that not all brief-service programmes are geared exclusively to brief service, nor are all brief therapy programmes oriented to a crisis framework.

Crisis intervention and brief psychotherapy

Many authors have wrestled with the elusive problem of differentiating "crisis intervention" from "short-term" dynamic psychotherapy. Marmor (1979), who considers brief therapy as the wave of the future, suggests that the goal of crisis intervention is to reduce stress and *sustain* the client's coping, thus helping the client recuperate enough to return to a precrisis state of functioning. In contrast, short-term dynamic therapy more ambitiously *modifies* the patient's ability to cope and focuses on "only secondarily relieving stress" (p154). Mindful that "there are no sharp lines of demarcation" and that "each can merge into the other", Marmor pursues his inquiry:

"Emergency treatment may proceed from the provision of immediate relief to an effort to reduce the precipitating stress situation, and in crisis intervention it is often necessary to help the patient develop more effective coping mechanisms to deal with the presenting stress situation as well as future ones. To the extent that crisis intervention emphasises the modification of coping mechanisms it moves closer to short-term dynamic psychotherapy. The differences are primarily in terms of emphasis. Crisis intervention is usually of shorter duration and limited to five or six sessions and dynamic psychotherapy is usually of longer duration. The primary goal of crisis intervention is the restoration of homeostasis. A secondary goal is to improve the patient's adaptive capacity when necessary. The basic goal of short-term dynamic psychotherapy is to improve the patient's coping abilities. The termination point of crisis intervention is when the crisis is resolved. The termination point of short-term dynamic therapy is not dictated by the resolution of the crisis. Crisis intervention involves a more supportive approach than does short-term dynamic psychotherapy. It can also be more directive. In short-term dynamic therapy, the approach is active but nondirective. Crisis intervention deals only with the here and now; short-term dynamic psychotherapy includes the exploration of the past to illuminate the present. Finally crisis intervention may involve a variety of other techniques (e.g., family therapy, group therapy, and dealing with the social network), but short-term dynamic psychotherapy is essentially a one-to-one approach. However, it may well be that the lessons learned from short-term dynamic psychotherapy will find increasing application in conjoint marital, family, and group therapies as time goes on." (p154).

Marmor is quoted in detail because his inquiry suggests a *continuum* or *blending* of methods of therapy (from support and relief of stressful symptoms to in-depth attempts to alter basic coping mechanisms, including "exploration of the past to illuminate the present") rather than a *dichotomy* of crisis intervention versus brief dynamic therapy. To the extent, then, that crisis therapists try to help clients in the crucible of crisis to alter basic personality patterns and coping styles, their "technique clearly merges into short-term dynamic psychotherapy and differs from it primarily in being of shorter duration and crisis oriented" (Marmor, 1979, p154, footnote).

Thus, according to this definition, our brief crisis intervention approach, structured within a flexible time frame of, say, from six to twenty interviews (including one or two preplanned follow-ups), is equivalent in scope to "short-term psychotherapy". The practitioner's orientation may, as indicated below, be primarily psychodynamic, behavioural, cognitive, existential, or a prudent integrative blend of two or more of these approaches. By "prudent" we mean that the therapist's approach is based on the client's needs rather than on the therapist's ideological predilections.

Importance in human services

Why is crisis intervention important in the field of human services? This question can be answered by referring to the universality of human experience with life crises causing disruption in people's ability to cope. Crises occur wherever there are people - at home, at school, at work, or at leisure. Informal crisis counselling is usually part of everybody's personal, family, and social functioning in the sense that we help each other by listening, encouraging, and giving information and advice during acutely stressful periods. When offered by trained, sensitive caregivers and professionals, crisis intervention services can be of special importance. People in crisis predicaments are often amenable to preventive, protective, and corrective influences because by definition their defences are lower during the high-anxiety stages of most crisis experiences than they are before or after a crisis when defences are in place and they are thus less motivated to change. To cite Bloom (1980) "an hour spent with the client at the time of the crisis has the same potential benefit as perhaps ten hours spent with that same client after the enhanced state of readiness to change has passed" (p114).

Through prompt and effective intervention, practitioners can help prevent the development of more serious psychosocial problems that often occur after the crisis or emergency is over if the crisis is maladaptively rather than adaptively resolved. Hence, the last four chapters of our sourcebook (Parad & Parad, 1990) focus on preventive interventions. Most crisis intervention experiences are classified by mental health experts as early secondary prevention. Certain protective interventions, for example, on behalf of children who are potentially at risk but who have shown no obvious signs of difficulty, may be classified as primary prevention. Still other corrective intervention procedures, because they are utilised some time after the onset of the original problem, may be classified as tertiary prevention. Thus crisis intervention services serve both preventive and remedial purposes; they may well strengthen the person's ability to learn from the crisis experience and offer the individual opportunities for growth. Ideally, they prevent or at the very least help reduce human suffering and pain at times of illness, bereavement, divorce, disaster, or other severe stress.

Historical background

This section provides a selective overview of theoretical, programme, legislative, and research developments in the evolution of contemporary crisis intervention in the USA. It is not intended as a comprehensive chronicle of the use of the crisis concept or of time limits in the mental health professions and social and behavioural sciences. There are many contributions from psychiatry, social work, psychology, and sociology to crisis theory.

The roots of crisis intervention may be traced to several sources. During World War II and the Korean and the Vietnam wars mental health professionals learned that soldiers suffering from combat fatigue (now called post-traumatic stress disorder) were more likely to be returned to combat duty if they were treated at or near the front lines by immediate brief therapy, thus avoiding regression and secondary gain as well as feelings of failure and guilt about abandoning their buddies (Menninger, 1948; Glass, 1954; Laufer, Frey-Wouters & Gallops, 1985). The rationale for emergency military psychiatry - similar to today's crisis intervention approach - included the general expectation that the traumatised soldier would soon recompensate and return to active duty if given prompt, supportive therapy with opportunity to ventilate and debrief; reassurance that his symptoms were typical of persons exposed to extreme stress; and proper medication, if needed. It was found that soldiers who were permanently withdrawn from front-line assignments also experienced loss of peer group support, which aggravated their sense of stigma about being a psychiatric casualty.

Lindemann's (1944) classic study of the bereaved disaster victims of a 1942 fire in the Coconut Grove nightclub in Boston was a pioneering contribution to the development of preventive crisis intervention for persons who are unlikely to cope appropriately with the crisis of bereavement. In 1948 Lindemann organised an innovative community mental health programme, the Wellesley Human Relations Service, where his colleagues, Gerald Caplan, Donald Klein (Klein & Lindemann, 1961) and others, stimulated research on primary prevention relating to school entry and other life-cycle transitions (Klein & Ross, 1958).

Although the foundation work was done by Lindemann, Caplan is generally acknowledged as the master architect of preventive crisis intervention. In 1954, under the aegis of the Harvard University School of Public Health, Caplan established the Harvard Family Guidance Centre, a multidisciplinary crisis research and consultation project to study the impact of four stressors - premature birth, birth of children with congenital anomalies, birth of twins, and tuberculosis - on ordinary families in a lower - and working-class area of Boston. As the social work member of this mental health-public health team, Howard Parad went beyond the project's research focus to explore and elaborate experimental techniques for preventive and corrective (early secondary) crisis intervention (Parad, 1961), with consultation from Caplan (Parad & Caplan, 1960).

Caplan's metatheory of preventive psychiatry provided much of the rationale for the community mental health ideology of that era (Caplan, 1964). The Harvard Family Guidance Centre and its successor, the Harvard Laboratory of Community Psychiatry, trained leaders in community-oriented psychiatry, psychology, social work, and nursing who, like itinerant preachers, travelled throughout the United States and abroad to spread the gospel of community mental health in general and crisis intervention in particular (Schulberg & Killilea, 1982). A succession of studies concerned with a broad range of health and situational crises and their implications for individual and family functioning as well as for preventive crisis intervention and crisis consultation were initiated.

Though sometimes ignored in reviews of crisis intervention, Bellak's contributions to brief emergency psychotherapy (BEP) are important (Bellak & Siegel, 1983). In 1958, Bellak started the first psychiatric emergency twenty-four hours walk-in clinic in the United States - the Trouble-Shooting Clinic at Elmhurst City Hospital in New York. Based primarily on psychodynamic theory, the BEP approach borrowed selectively from learning and systems theories and was limited to five sessions plus follow-up. While focusing on the patient's crisis predicament, the BEP

11

therapist also attended to the "establishment of causality - of continuity between the present and the past" (Bellak & Siegel, 1983 p3).

A few years later, in 1962, Jacobson, influenced by Caplan's theories, launched the Benjamin Rush Centre for Problems in Living in Los Angeles. Annually serving approximately 1,750 persons in crisis, the centre has been part of the Didi Hirsch Community Mental Health Centre (Jacobson, 1980) since 1975. A walk-in clinic, it offers up to six sessions (the number used by most crisis clinics) to individuals and families coping with life crises.

The Quick Response Unit of Jewish Family Service of New York City provides a more recent example of an innovative crisis programme combining the following components: Prompt response to the cry for help, flexible use of time limits (up to six sessions) and spacing of interviews, selective use of home visits, involvement of significant others, and mobilisation of social resources (Goldring, 1980).

In the United States, national and state legislation further accelerated the need for experimentation to more effectively provide emergency mental health and crisis services, including:

1. The provision in the 1963 Community Mental Health Centres Act (PL-88-174) requiring twenty-four hour crisis or emergency services as one of the five compulsory programme features in community mental health centres financed under this landmark legislation.
2. Policy decisions to depopulate state mental hospitals, thus emphasising services for the client or patient in his or her own community. The decision to deinstitutionalise challenged the resources of many communities as well as the tolerance threshold of many families, as the number of patients discharged increased. The discharged patient, who all too often is dismissed from the state hospital without the support of an adequate aftercare plan, therefore often decompensates and requires crisis intervention services.
3. The Emergency Medical Services System Act of 1973, providing guidelines for medical and psychological emergencies.
4. The Crisis Counselling Assistance and Training Section of the Federal Disaster Relief Act of 1974 (42 USC-5183), providing funds from the National Institute of Mental Health for brief crisis services to disaster victims as well as short-term training activities - often sponsored by the Red Cross and other rescue organisations - for crisis workers to staff one-stop disaster aid centres.

Summary

In summary, during the past thirty years, the concepts of dynamic ego psychology, crisis-inducing stress, planned use of time limits, task-oriented problem solving, and emergency mental health have been operationalised in both experimental and ongoing crisis intervention programs (often facilitated by the above-mentioned legislation) to rapidly meet the needs of people experiencing interpersonal, maturational, and situational crisis and to better utilise mental health personnel in a cost-effective manner.

The proliferation of innovative, planned, short-term treatment services may generally be said to have coincided with the emergence of a rationale - namely, the crisis approach. Because, as earlier stated, most crises are time-limited, crisis intervention provided both a rationale and a method for use in brief treatment. Although during the 1960's crisis intervention helped provide planned short-term treatment (PSTT) with a conceptual and programme rationale, during the 1970's and 1980's systematic experimentally designed research on the favourable cost effectiveness of PSTT gave crisis intervention increasing credibility. It is also interesting to note that Taft's early formulation of time as a key factor in the therapeutic process, which previously was dismissed due to the professional imbroglio of the Freudians versus the Rankians ("functionalist" social workers influenced by Otto Rank's theories of separation, time, choice and will), could now be reinvigorated and integrated with the crisis intervention framework that emerged in the 1960's (Taft, 1933; Parad & Parad, 1968).

The following interrelated developments contributed to the widespread acceptance of crisis-oriented, brief-treatment approaches: Research on precipitating stress and coping behaviour; the imbalance between high demand for therapeutic services and scarce resources; recurrent personnel and financial restraints, including the reluctance of many insurance companies to reimburse therapy vendors for long-term treatment; continued emphasis on accountability and related cost/benefit issues; studies of crisis intervention services to certain ethnic groups; the contributions of the newer cognitive, behavioural, humanistic, and eclectic perspectives regarding problem-solving and action-oriented coping repertoires; and the accelerated interest in family therapy. The burgeoning interest of crisis intervention personnel in nonkinship networks and other social systems, reflected in their thinking about the crisis experience in the context of community social supports, has also been important.

Practice applications

When does the practitioner use crisis techniques? The pragmatic answer is whenever there is an event that precipitates a significant upset in a steady state. Thus crisis intervention has wide applicability and in many programmes is the preferred mode of service delivery, as indicated in the chapters of this volume.

In brief, the crisis-oriented therapist should be attuned to three questions. These questions are, of course, relevant to all intake procedures: What is troubling the client? Why does he or she come for help now? What can I do to help? The first two questions concern the client's presenting problem and his or her perception of the crisis-inducing stress, and the third question concerns the actual methods of clinical intervention. These principles and techniques are substantially the same as those used in long-term therapy, but they require certain modifications in approach and

13

emphasis. Specifically, the therapist changes his or her technique by assuming a more active role in order to foster the client's cognitive awareness of realistic aspects of the stressful situation as well as to avoid regression in the client and to promote mastery within a brief period. The crisis therapist is more likely than are other therapists to give advice, make disciplined use of confrontation techniques, and to use focused rather than diffuse interviewing techniques.

Crisis therapy also accepts and emphasises limited but significant clear-cut goals more readily than does traditional, open-ended treatment. Techniques of role rehearsal or anticipatory guidance help clients prepare for stressful situations that they are likely to encounter between interviews or after therapy had ended. Homework assignments (for example, keeping a log of critical incidents, checking a community resource, talking with a significant other), similar to those used in task-centred PSTT, are often given to enhance (1) problem-solving between sessions and (2) the client's sense of mastery and accompanying sense of self-esteem.

During the crisis-resolution period, the client often needs the support of community resources and services to relieve environmental pressures that trigger or aggravate the crisis situation. Thus, it must be emphasised that the full benefits of crisis intervention programmes can be realised on a long-range basis only when supplemented by adequate community-support systems. Ideally, these include homemaker and legal-aid services; employment and job training opportunities; income maintenance provisions; a range of housing resources (including independent living, halfway house, crisis hostel, foster care and other residential facilities geared to the individual's rehabilitation potential); and involvement of families and significant others in the person's social network (Rueveni, 1975). In addition, mentally disordered persons * often need appropriate, medically supervised psychotropic medication.

It is also important to utilise adventitious influences that may enhance the therapeutic process, for example, the client's tendency to invest trust and hopeful expectancy in the therapist, often an aspect of positive transference (Frank, 1973). The crisis clinician must be aware of a person's self-help resources and the fact that these natural self-healing efforts are often efficacious.

The crisis counsellor's basic task is to help clients change those affective (feeling), cognitive (thinking), and behavioural (doing) patterns that hinder effective value clarification and rule making as well as to encourage constructive communication and appropriate role behaviour. Thus it is essential to develop a judiciously eclectic approach that attends to these domains of human functioning (feeling, thinking and doing) in order to help persons in crisis mobilise the resources that will unblock and enhance performance in these vital areas.

* For further information see Chapter 10, Howard J. Parad & Libbie G. Parad (eds.) (1990) *Crisis Intervention Book 2: The Practitioner's Sourcebook for Brief Therapy* Milwaukee, Wi.: Family Service America.

Because attention is concentrated on the client's current problem in functioning rather than on less immediately relevant childhood antecedents, history taking should be selective in relation to key derivative conflicts. However, a caveat is in order: The crisis clinician should actively explore the connection between the client's current impasse and analogous events, activated by the present crisis, from the recent as well as the remote past. These past events may well represent previous unresolved life crises that the client now has a second chance to resolve adaptively because his or her defences are more fluid during the "hot" crisis response phase than they will be when the crisis is over. The following case from a crisis clinic dramatically illustrates (1) how the present crisis turmoil may reflect the derepression of unresolved childhood crises and (2) the opportunities for eclectically oriented interventions:

Mrs. A, a thirty-four year old obese woman, visited a walk-in crisis clinic in a panicky state at the urging of her sister. She couldn't stop crying, was "going around in circles", and couldn't get anything done at home. She wanted help because she and her husband were quarrelling about unpaid bills. That morning Mr. A left the house and said he would spent the night at a friend's apartment; he had never done this before. Mr. A worked as a carpenter for a local contractor. The couple had three children, ages twelve, eleven and nine. They had been arguing about bills for several weeks. Several days previously, in desperation, Mrs. A pawned Mr. A's shotgun to help pay bills. A few weeks earlier, in the course of one of their fights about money, Mr. A had threatened his wife with the shotgun.

Mrs. A stated that for the past few months she had been unable to take the mail out of the mailbox. When the mail, including bills, was removed by her husband she was afraid to open and read it, so it was usually left unopened on the dining room table. Hence bills did not get paid. Each person seemed to expect the other to do something about their budget problems.

For the past two months, Mrs. A had had a strange repetitive dream* about a casket. She recalled that when she was six, her father, then thirty-five, died suddenly in an accident caused by his drunkenness. (She had been very scared when, at the funeral, her mother had, in reality, told her to kiss her father in the casket.) She had not told her "weird" dream to anyone but the worker because she was scared of her husband's reactions. The casket in the dream reminded her of her mailbox. In three weeks, her husband would be thirty-five. Thinking about his birthday made her anxious. She didn't know why. Crying, she asked for help in getting her husband to return home.

* For an extended discussion of the use of dreams in short-term dynamic crisis-oriented therapy see Howard J. Parad & Libbie G. Parad (eds.) (1990) *Crisis Intervention Book 2: The Practitioner's Sourcebook for Brief Therapy* Milwaukee, Wi.: Family Service America.

Imagining that we are the intake crisis counsellor, let us briefly sketch Mr. & Mrs. A's situation from the perspective of the stress-crisis configuration:

1. *Precipitating stressor(s):* The immediate triggering event (the "last straw") is Mr. A's threat not to return, preceded by (a) tense quarrels about unpaid bills, (b) Mr. A's disturbing homicidal threat to shoot his wife, and (c) Mrs. A's impulsive pawning of Mr. A's shotgun. Mindful of the difficulty in untangling cause from effect in this not atypical concatenation of domestic disputes, we can at least agree that the above three events represent predisposing stress factors (or "hazardous events").

2. *Perception of stressors:* Panicky, crying, her routines disrupted, Mrs. A clearly feels threatened by the possible loss of her husband's presence in the home, not to mention her surfacing preconscious fear that he may suffer an untimely death, as did her father. Mr. A. we can safely speculate, is furious over the pawning of his shotgun, which he may perceive as a threat to his manliness and status in the family.

3. *Crisis response:* In light of these perceptions, Mrs. A suddenly experiences crisis. Mr. A is probably also experiencing crisis. The typical signs of an active crisis state manifested by Mrs. A are that she can't stop crying and she's immobilised at home - going around in circles. Without seeing Mr. A (he should be involved in treatment, if possible), the counsellor may assume that his impulsive departure, which never occurred before, is a sign of crisis and perhaps a cry for help.

4. *Crisis resolution:* Obviously, it is important that the crisis counsellor see Mrs. A. immediately, consistent with our emphasis on early-access treatment. Of course, intervention choices flow from the counsellor's prompt assessment, which is that the couple appears to have a reasonably viable though strained relationship. Using a direct approach, the counsellor assures Mrs. A that her dream is very important, while appreciating how frightening it is to her. Although the dream seems "weird", the counsellor understands that it relates to her anxiety about her husband's impending birthday.

The counsellor might speculate (privately) about oedipal remnants if so inclined (Gardner, 1958). The trauma of her father's death, the counsellor later learns, was compounded by Mrs. A's removal to the home of relatives (so she wouldn't be upset!) immediately after the funeral. This dramatic example of an erupting anniversary syndrome reflects considerable derepression of long-denied bereavement affects, with mounting tension and anxiety about the possible death of her loved/feared/hated husband.

To foster Mrs. A's coping, the counsellor directs Mrs. A to call her husband and tell him about her scary dream . Her sister, who is present for part of the interview, thinks this is a good idea, because Mr. & Mrs. A have a pretty good marriage. The suggestion works: Mr. A listens, not too sympathetically. Thus the couple re-establish contact (which was the worker's goal), and

Mr. A returns home.

In the next session, Mrs.A exclaims with tearful agony. "So that's why I don't get the bills from the mailbox - it reminds me of my father's casket in the dream". (The mailbox is of the large "rural delivery" type.) "I'm scared my husband will die when he becomes thirty-five!"

Thus, by affording Mrs. A an opportunity for ventilation and catharsis, and by encouraging her to restore communication with her husband, the counsellor helps the couple rapidly achieve equilibrium over a period of four sessions. However, serious unresolved problems obviously remain: The unpaid bills, Mrs. A's threat to use the shotgun, Mrs. A's partially resolved grief regarding her father's traumatic death, Mrs. A's obesity, and Mr. A's tendency to avoid dealing with financial and emotional issues. Thus this case illustrates both the efficacy and limits of very brief (fewer than six sessions) crisis intervention.

An eclectically skilled therapist would have had the option of treating Mrs. A's phobic reaction to the mailbox through systematic desensitisation techniques (guided imagery, muscle relaxation) if the cathartic ventilation used in the crisis counsellor's psychodynamic approach had failed to produce quick relief. It is also important to note that according to systematic comparisons of brief behavioural and psychodynamic therapies, symptom substitution, a response often feared by psychodynamic therapists when behaviour modification is used, does *not* occur in a statistically significant manner (Sloane, Staples, Cristol, Yorkston & Whipple, 1975; Wachtel, 1977).

Flushed with enthusiasm about his apparently successful intervention, the relatively inexperienced crisis counsellor neglected to plan a follow-up with Mrs. A that, ideally, would involve Mr. A. Such a follow-up would have been more desirable than his simply suggesting that Mrs. A "feel free to call if things don't go well around the time of your husband's birthday". Planned follow-ups - in person, if possible, by telephone, if not - serve three important purposes: (a) They offer a safeguard against undue arbitrariness in structuring time limits - the door should be open for further help or referral if needed, (b) they afford the crisis clinic a chance to get valuable feedback from the client concerning the actual crisis outcome (better than precrisis state? about the same? or worse?); and (c) they offer the crisis clinician an opportunity to bolster and reinforce the client's confidence and future coping ability. Thus, planned follow-ups, anticipated with the client well before the case is closed, should be a vital component of all crisis programmes. Although Mann (1973) sternly warns that follow-up sessions should not be mentioned to the client until just before they are conducted, other clinicians who have done preplanned follow-ups have not experienced the disastrous consequences predicted by Mann.

To return to Mrs. A., the counsellor should have considered the possibility of referring Mrs. A. to a self-help weight-reduction group and to a family counselling agency for aid in budget management. Linkage with self-help and other community support groups (for example,

Alcoholics Anonymous, Adult Children of Alcoholics, Recovery Inc.), often helps clients maintain, even enhance, postcrisis functioning (Langsley & Kaplan, 1968). Finally, although there was a good result, Mr. A should have been included in the intervention.

Space limitations do not permit further explication of the components of an eclectic/pluralistic/interactional/perspective which we clearly favour. A crisis is an interpersonal or collective as well as an individual phenomenon in that it can be experienced by both family and nonkinship groups. Thus, the following are pertinent: Family therapy, group crisis counselling, intergenerational therapy, and involvement of significant others in the "social surround" of the client or patient. These include selected family members, fellow workers and supervisors in Employee Assistance Programmes (EAP's), other caregivers (for example, physicians, nurses, teachers, friends), and indeed anyone who is important to the person or persons experiencing a crisis.

Unfortunately, interactional and group crisis counselling are not sufficiently utilised in most mental health settings.* These methods offer exciting treatment possibilities in that they have been found to be an effective and economical tool for helping people who are experiencing similar life or work crises. Research increasingly indicates that interactional therapies, including couple, family and small-group approaches, are generally more effective in dealing with clients' problems in social functioning than are purely individual-centred approaches (Gurman & Kniskern, 1981).

A look into the future

As earlier indicated, crisis intervention is no longer the experimental fad many considered it to be thirty years ago. This international conference attests to that fact. Thus, we predict that in years to come brief crisis intervention will be regarded not only as a generally accepted but also as *a preferred mode* of delivering mental health services to clients under stress. Just as brief crisis treatment is now the method of choice at most university student counselling services, so, too, similar adaptations of time-limited crisis-oriented therapy for persons in stress are likely to be increasingly regarded as the treatment of choice in mental health programmes for children, adolescents, and adults (including the ageing) in a variety of child guidance, family service, hospital, and clinic settings.

Experimentation with brief crisis therapy will continue in many other settings such as child-care centres; employee assistance programmes in the workplace; and schools, where the need for brief individual, family, and group crisis counselling will grow as school enrolments rise.

In light of the accelerated interest in family and group therapy and

---

* For further discussion of interactional approaches (including family, intergenerational and group crisis counselling) see Howard J. Parad & Libbie G. Parad (eds.) (1990) *Crisis Intervention, Book 2: The Practitioner's Sourcebook for Brief Therapy* Milwaukee, Wi.: Family Service America.

the accompaning recognition of the role played by significant others in crisis resolution, the crisis counsellor of the future will probably be increasingly oriented to innovative interactional and network approaches. We hope that mental health workers dealing with health crises in hospitals will have flexible work schedules so they can do more family crisis therapy with family members and significant others during evening visitation hours when family members are likely to visit the patient in crisis. Because of their vital role as caregivers at times of crisis, police, firefighters, disaster aid workers, paramedic rescue workers, and similar personnel dealing with large numbers of people under stress will play an increasingly important role as crisis counsellors. They will need further training and consultation by professionals experienced in crisis intervention.

As economic restraints become tighter, cost-benefit requirements will ensure that brief therapy, approximately six to sixteen sessions in length, will be the wave of the future. Although not all brief therapy is crisis-oriented, many clients receiving brief therapy will be under severe stress and their therapists must be knowledgeable about crisis intervention.

Dramatic reports on drug abuse, sexual molestation, child and spousal abuse, and teenage suicide in the media will draw heightened public attention to these crisis experiences, creating further demand for around-the-clock hotline crisis intervention telephone services.

Increases in the population of older adults, combined with the growing sophistication of life-support medical technology, will further enhance the importance of sensitive crisis intervention and crisis consultation services to patients, their families, and medical personnel, all of whom are dealing with death and dying, often making agonising life-and-death decisions about whether to maintain or withdraw mechanical life-support systems.

In the future, time-limited crisis intervention will be taught as an integral part of graduate mental health courses on psychotherapy and counselling, rather than as a separate course.

In addition to the foregoing trends, which we feel have reasonable likelihood of coming to pass, we would like to offer several hopes for the future.

We hope that the practice of preventive crisis intervention will attract more attention from mental health professionals.

We hope that, despite the economic constraints plaguing researchers today, a renewed thrust to engage in systematic, rigorous research will engender a more precise, cumulative literature on the processes, outcomes, limits, and possible misuses of brief crisis intervention services. Knowledge regarding the structuring of time in crisis intervention needs to be refined. What is the optimal number of sessions for typical clients in crisis? What are the uses and limits of the single-session crisis interview? Is six still the modal number of sessions in most crisis intervention programmes?

A number of other topics deserve special attention: Criteria for different types of interventions with diverse ethnic groups; how the client and worker actually perceive and relate to time-structuring procedures;

the risks and advantages of crisis induction, a technique used by some professionals to accelerate change; specific ways in which eclectic action-therapy techniques (for example, psychodrama and sculpting) can be blended with other, more traditional approaches; how to deal with impasses in brief crisis therapy when the usual task-centred, problem-solving techniques don't work; better understanding of the common and specific therapeutic elements that contribute to a successful outcome; the costs and benefits of prearranged follow-up interviews and the differing effectiveness of individual, family and group crisis modalities. Also needed are carefully controlled experimental studies of open-ended versus time-limited crisis intervention approaches.

Conclusion

The crisis intervention approach advocated here requires certain administrative procedures to ensure that services are easily and promptly accessible and to provide for clients' needs rather than for the social agency's or clinic's convenience. A number of steps must be taken to meet these goals of proximity, accessibility, and effectiveness: (a) The virtual elimination of waiting lists (in part through the proper utilisation of professional and paraprofessional personnel); (b) the avoidance of complex intake screening so that psychosocial treatment will be virtually simultaneous with diagnosis; (c) the development of an open-door policy for persons who may require further services when faced with new unmanageable crises; (d) as previously indicated, the use of a built-in policy of preplanned follow-up interviews (by telephone, if necessary, for reasons of economic expedience) to provide feedback about the effectiveness of service, and to provide ethical safeguards when an arbitrary number of interviews is used in planned, short-term treatment arrangements; and (e) although this position may be controversial, wherever possible, the avoidance of centralised intake, which requires that clients be transferred to another staff member after their initial presentation of their crisis quandaries. Therapists should attempt to imagine how they would feel if they told their intimate story to a strange person, then, having developed some initial trust in a helping relationship, were required to tell their story to a new therapist.

Basic to implementation of these recommendations is an administrative mind-set that favours egalitarian rather than purely hierarchical arrangements among interdisciplinary staff members; encourages experimentation with interactional as opposed to purely individual-centred interviews; provides support to counsellors in order to avoid staff burnout (especially important in hotline, protective, and other emergency crisis services for high-risk populations); values disciplined, integrative eclecticism; believes in accountability for the effectiveness of services; and above all, respects the special vulnerabilities and strengths of people in crisis.

To summarize, we believe crisis intervention will be increasingly utilised in both traditional and non-traditional settings; it will be theoretically and technically *eclectic,* integrating psychodynamic, cognitive, behavioural, humanistic, and existential perspectives; it will be *interactionally oriented* to include significant others; it will be *preventive* in scope; and we hope, it will routinely include *systematic follow-up* studies to investigate the pros and cons of its effectiveness with diverse populations at risk.

Given the financial limitations within which mental health professionals now operate, it is unlikely that many comprehensive rigorous research efforts will be mounted in the near future, though the need for systematic research is urgent. However, even in the absence of such research, it is clear that crisis intervention is now an established component of ongoing services in most mental health and social welfare programmes. It is here to stay and it will grow, we hope, in a way that relieves suffering and maximises human potential throughout the world.

REFERENCES

AUERBACH, S. & STOLBERG, A. (eds.) (1986) *Crisis Intervention with Children and Families* Washington, DC: Hemisphere Publishing

BELLAK, L. & SIEGEL, H. (1983) *Handbook of Intensive Brief and Emergency Psychotherapy* Larchmont, NY: C.P.S. Inc.

BLOOM, B.L. (1980) Social and Community Interventions *Annual Review of Psychology* **31**:111-142.

BLOOM, B.L. (1981) Focused Single-Session Therapy: Initial Development and Evaluation. In: S.H. Budman (ed.) *Forms of Brief Therapy* New York: Guilford Press.

BUDMAN, S.D. & GURMAN, A. (1988) *Theory and Practice of Brief Therapy* New York: Guilford Press.

CAPLAN, G. (1964) *Principles of Preventive Psychiatry* New York: Basic Books.

FRANK, J.D. (1973) *Persuasion and Healing* Baltimore, MD: Johns Hopkins University Press.

GARDNER, G. (1958) The Balanced Expression of Oedipal Remnants. In: H.J. Parad (ed.) *Ego Psychology and Dynamic Casework* New York: Family Service Association of America.

GLASS, A. (1954) Psychotherapy in the Combat Zone *American Journal of Psychiatry* **110**:725-731.

GOLDRING, J. (1980). *Quick Response Therapy: A Time-Limited Treatment Approach*. New York: Human Sciences Press.

GURMAN, A. & KNISKERN, D. (eds.) (1981) *Handbook of Family Therapy* New York: Brunner/Mazel.

HILL, R. (1965) Generic Features of Families under Stress. In: H.J. Parad (ed.) *Crisis Intervention: Selected Readings* New York: Family Service Association of America.

HOROWITZ, M.J. (1986) *Stress-Response Syndromes* New York: Jason Aronson.

HOROWITZ, M.J. & Kaltreider, N.B. (1980) Brief Treatment of Post-Traumatic Stress Disorders. In: G. Jacobson (ed.) *Crisis Intervention in the 80's* San Francisco: Jossey-Bass.

JACOBSON, G. (1980). Crisis Theory. In: G. Jacobson (ed.) *Crisis Intervention in the 80's* San Francisco: Jossey-Bass.

KAGAN, R. & SCHLOSBERG, S. (1989) *Families in Perpetual Crisis* New York: W.W. Norton.

KLEIN, D. & LINDEMANN, E. (1961) Preventive Intervention in Individual and Family Crisis Situations. In: G. Caplan (ed.) *Prevention of Mental Disorders in Children* New York: Basic Books.

KLEIN, D. & ROSS, A. (1958) Kindergarten Entry: A Study of Role Transition. In: M. Krugman (ed.) *Orthopsychiatry and the School* New York: American Orthopsychiatric Association.

LANGSLEY, D. & KAPLAN, D. (1968) *Treatment of Families in Crisis* New York: Grune & Stratton.

LAUFER, R.; FREY-WOUTERS, E. & GALLOPS, M.S. (1985) Traumatic Stressors in the Vietnam War and Post-Traumatic Stress Disorder. In: C. Figley (ed.) *Trauma and its Wake* New York: Brunner/Mazel.

LINDEMANN, E. (1944) Symptomatology and Management of Acute Grief *American Journal of Psychiatry,* **101** (September). Also in: H.J. Parad (ed.) (1965) *Crisis Intervention: Selected Readings* New York: Family Service Association of America.

LINDEMANN, E. (1956) The Meaning of Crisis in Individual and Family Living *Teachers College Record* **57**:310-315.

MANN, J. (1973) *Time-Limited Psychotherapy* Cambridge, MA: Harvard University Press.

MARMOR, J. (1979) Short-term Dynamic Psychotherapy *American Journal Of Psychiatry* **136**:149-155.

McCUBBIN, H. & PATTERSON, J. (1983) Family Transitions: Adaptations to Stress. In: H. McCubbin & C. Figley (eds.) *Stress and the Family, Vol 1* New York: Brunner/Mazel.

MENNINGER, W.C. (1948). *Psychiatry in a Troubled World* New York: Macmillan.

PARAD, H.J. (1961) *Preventive Casework: Problems and Implications* Social
Welfare Forum   New York: Columbia University Press.

PARAD, H.J. (ed.) (1965) *Crisis Intervention: Selected Readings* New York:
Family Service Association of America.

PARAD, H.J. (1977) Crisis Intervention. In: *Encyclopaedia of Social Work*
Washington, DC: National Association of Social Workers.

PARAD, H.J. (1982) Brief Family Therapy. In: H.Schulberg & M. Killilea (eds.).
*The Modern Practice of Community Mental Health: A Volume in Honour of
Gerald Caplan* San Francisco: Jossey-Bass.

PARAD, H.J. & CAPLAN, G. (1960) A Framework for Studying Families in Crisis
Social Work **5**:3-15 Also in H.J. Parad, Ed.), (1965) *Crisis Intervention: Selected
Readings*. New York: Family Service Association of America.

PARAD, H.J. & PARAD, L.G. (eds.) (1990) *Crisis Intervention Book 2: The
Practitioner's Sourcebook for Brief Therapy* Milwaukee, Wi: Family Service
America.

PARAD, L.G. (1971) Short Term Treatment: An Overview of Historical Trends,
Issues and Potentials *Smith College Studies in Social Work* **41**: 1971, 119-146.

PARAD, L.G. & PARAD, H.J. (1968) A Study of Crisis-Oriented Short-Term
Treatment *Social Casework* **49**:418-426.

RUEVENI, V. (1975) Network Intervention with a Family in Crisis *Family Process*
14:193-204.

SCHULBERG, H. & KILLILEA, M. (eds.) (1982) *The Modern Practice of Community
Mental Health: A Volume in Honour of Gerald Caplan* San Francisco: Jossey-
Bass.

SLOANE, R.B.; STAPLES, F.R. CRISTOL, A.H.; YORKSTON, N.J. & WHIPPLE, K. (1975)
Psychotherapy versus Behaviour Therapy Cambridge, MA: Harvard University
Press.

TAFT, J. (1933) *The Dynamics of Therapy in a Controlled Relationship* New
York: Macmillan.

VAN HOOK, M. (1987) Harvest of Despair: Using the ABCX Model for Farm
Families in Crisis *Social Casework* **68**:273-278.

WACHTEL, P. (1977) *Psychoanalysis and Behaviour Therapy: Toward an
Integration* New York: Basic Books.

Crisis Intervention in Practice - An International Perspective

N. Rao Punukollu

Introduction

After outlining the concepts of crisis theory and its application in psychiatric practice, a description is made on how Crisis Intervention approach is being practised in different parts of the world. Crisis theory is applied in various settings, but this article is primarily concerned with the application of Crisis theory in the management of psychiatric emergencies (Lindemann, 1944) in different parts of the world.

What is crisis?

Crisis is defined as a response to external or internal stress which cannot be managed by the usual coping mechanisms of the person stressed. A crisis occurs "when an individual faced with an obstacle to important life goals, finds that it is for the time being insurmountable through the utilisation of customary problem solving methods" (Caplan, 1964). The person and the family affected by the crisis go through three phases:

Phase I: leads to rise of tension, anxiety and failure of habitual solving mechanisms.

Phase II: leads to increased rise in tension and disorganisation. This is the period of maximum susceptibility to change. In this phase regression occurs and the person in crisis would be able to ventilate the conflicts that are causing the distress in their life.

Phase III: leads to exhaustion and psychic disorganisation. In this phase people could show psychotic features and may lack reality and orientation.

Skilled therapeutic intervention in phase II
(24 hours - 2 weeks)

During Phase II, crisis therapists have considerable scope to help the individual and the family affected with crisis. During this period minimal intervention can have maximum impact. Crisis therapy can provide an opportunity for individuals in crisis to learn new constructive coping strategies to resolve their crisis.

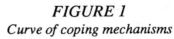

FIGURE 1
Curve of coping mechanisms

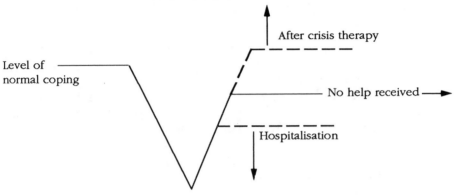

As outlined in Figure 1, each person has a normal level of coping which may vary at different times in their life. When a crisis occurs this level rapidly falls down. The recovery period from this stage of regression back to normality varies depending on what strategies the individual and the family have adopted. If the person does not receive any help, it is possible the person may recover back to the previous levels of coping or it is possible that s/he may adopt some maladaptive strategies for dealing with the stress, thereby reducing the previous levels of normal coping. If a person is hospitalised in a psychiatric ward, then the sick role is adopted, and reinforced by staff and relatives. The patient and family will not have the opportunity to learn new coping strategies. Hospitalisation also reduces self esteem and previous coping skills; encourages the sick role and regression; and leads to stigma and social breakdown. Psychosocial problems could be converted into a medical problem. If a person goes through this process of hospitalisation followed by return to the wider community, then s/he finds it more difficult to cope with any future crisis and consequently reseeks hospital admission, possibly becoming a "revolving door" patient.

As described in Figure 1, if the person undergoes crisis therapy by skilled crisis therapists, there is scope for the individual affected to learn new coping skills and constructive ways of coping. Crisis intervention teaches new coping skills and improves the coping mechanisms, so that one can resolve a future crisis without breaking down. Crisis intervention also helps the individual and the family not to adopt maladaptive coping strategies in dealing with the crisis.

FIGURE 2
Medical model versus psycho-social model

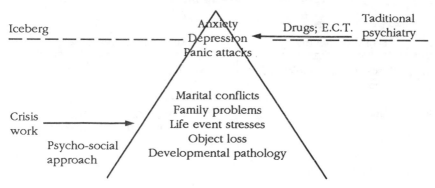

As described in Figure 2, in the traditional psychiatric medical model, symptoms are given primary importance in making a diagnosis and preparing a treatment plan. The traditional approach concentrates primarily on the symptoms. Symptomatic relief can be achieved by drugs, ECT or even by some psychotherapeutic methods such as relaxation techniques, behavioural approaches, etc. However, the crisis intervention approach concentrates on the real problems and will attempt to deal with these issues through the opportunity created by the crisis. The majority of the problems underlying psychiatric symptoms are really due to problems in relationships, family, marriage, life event stresses, object loss, developmental pathology, etc. During a period of crisis there is great scope for people to divulge long-held secrets and conflicts, which they have found very difficult to discuss or even to bring to their own conscious awareness in the past. This will give the individual an opportunity to overcome pain, by resolving the underlying conflicts. Crisis therapists practice with a psychosocial approach and the major emphasis is on real issues. Biological and medical approaches are also used for assessment and relief of symptoms, but would take a secondary role.

Crisis Therapy

Crisis therapy involves early intervention as crisis theory emphasises that Phase II is the sensitive period where minimal interventions have maximum impact on the individual and his or her family. The crisis therapist should be easily available and be able to respond quickly. Treatment should take place at the patients' own home so that crisis therapists can involve family, friends and neighbours where appropriate. Crisis therapy need the involvement of a persons' family and environment in order to understand the real issues leading to his or her present crisis. Consistent treatment by the same team with intensive regular follow-up on a daily basis is an essential part of crisis therapy.

FIGURE 3
Stages of crisis therapy

	Stages of therapy	Key worker's responses
1.	Assessment; formulation; hypothesis	Exciting
2.	Management plan	Stress creating; risk taking; responsibility; decision making; options; persistence
3.	Working through	Needs patience, persistence, hard work
4.	Critically evaluate: change plan if necessary	Critical, independent and creative thinking; keyworker ⇌ team
5.	Resolution	Satisfaction: confidence↑; self-esteem↑

Crisis therapy - Stages

As outlined in Figure 3, crisis intervention therapy can usefully be divided into five stages.

Stage 1   Assessment, Formulation and Hypothesis
This is the stage of "Assessment, Formulation and Hypothesis". Here, therapists need to look at the underlying issues of the iceberg and not limit themselves to the tip of the iceberg, i.e. symptoms. Hypothesis and formulation at this stage requires assessment of the individual and the family, and understanding of the environment. In crisis intervention therapy the first few interviews can be lengthy. It is necessary to develop a hypothesis at an early stage in order to formulate a management plan, as the early stages are the sensitive periods where minimal intervention will have maximum impact. Interviewing at this stage requires a good understanding of the conflicts involved and a correct hypothesis. This period is exciting to the crisis therapist as it involves exploration.

Stage II   Management Plan
Stage II involves the "Management Plan". Before reaching this stage the crisis therapists have already come to an understanding of the possible hypothesis and reasons for the conflicts underlying the current crisis. This stage is very stressful for crisis therapists as it

involves risk taking, responsibility and decision making. This
involves considering various options, and persistence.

Stage III   Working Through

This stage involves "Working Through". By this time the crisis
therapists have adopted a good Management Plan based on the
correct hypothesis. However, this needs patience, persistence and
hard work. Although we know what the real problem is, this does
not mean that the problem will disappear automatically. It needs
some time to work through. This particular period may not necessarily
be exciting but it requires hard work of a conscientious therapist,
persistently offering help to the individual and family affected in
order to overcome conflicts and to help them adopt correct coping
strategies for better mental health.

Stage IV   Critical Evaluation

This stage involves critical evaluation of the Management Plan and
the hypothesis if any new information arises which is not compatible
with the original formulation, or if the person or family demonstrate
limited or no response to treatment. It is necessary for the key
therapists to remain critical. It has been found that the team approach
is more effective in treating people in crisis (Ishikawa, 1991) than
an individual approach. Crisis teams could be used to help individual
therapists to understand the issues, prepare the hypothesis and
management plan, and to re-evaluate case management.

Stage V   Resolution

This is the final stage in which the person in crisis and their family
gain insight and resolve problems, learn new coping strategies and
eliminate symptoms. This is a period of "Resolution", which gives
great satisfaction and confidence to therapists and improves their
self-esteem. Therapists particularly feel great professional satisfaction
with community work compared to their past hospital ward
experiences. After working through a few cases the crisis therapist
gains more experience in managing the crisis effectively; after a few
years of managing such cases therapists may no longer feel very
stressed by the demands placed on them.

How crisis intervention is practised

Operational aspects of crisis intervention require easy availability of
the team members, by long-range bleeps or by other communication
systems so that they can be reached easily by the family and person in
crisis, and are therefore able to offer immediate aid. After this the team
needs to visit the family frequently, perhaps several times a day or on a
daily basis in the first two weeks, followed by frequent visits in the ensuing

weeks. Crisis intervention treatment involves both the patient and the family. The family requires information, support, guidance and counselling. It is essential that care is consistently given by one team and by named key workers. The reduction of tension by psychosocial and pharamacological means can be undertaken, as reduced tension levels enhance problem soling abilities. A preparedness to go out to both the patient and relatives assertively but without being unnecessarily intrusive is necessary. It is also essential that the team should be prepared to help with practical problems arising in the daily life of the family. Crisis intervention provides a service which is easily accessible, mobile and rapidly responsive, so that patients and relatives feel secure.

Psychiatric emergency room approach versus crisis approach

Crisis intervention approach differs from a traditional psychiatric approach in the handling of psychiatric emergencies. The traditional approach to psychiatric emergencies uses medical concepts whereby a patient is diagnosed medically and the emphasis of treatment is primarily on medication. Little significance is given to underlying conflicts and psychosocial problems. This approach would also not consider that crisis is an opportunity to learn new coping strategies. Psychiatric emergencies are traditionally dealt with in the same way as medical emergencies in a medical casualty room, and no consideration is given to the sensitive learning period during crisis situations.

The crisis intervention approach is primarily a psychosocial approach and views the crisis as a learning period, and as a period of opportunity to learn new coping strategies. Conversely, a crisis intervention approach is primarily psychosocial in orientation, and because crisis is viewed as a learning period, maximises the opportunities presented to learn new coping strategies.

Effects of crisis intervention

The crisis intervention team approach (a) prevents first time hospital admission and (b) if admitted, reduces the length of stay (Langsley, 1968). It teaches new coping strategies and reduces costs and stigma. It improves interaction in the family and helps understanding of the real conflicts. Crisis intervention treatment has been found to lead to good symptom remission and is considered satisfactory by both the patients and the relatives (Stein & Test, 1980). This last study also demonstrated that burden on carers was not increased.

Psychiatric emergency service in the U.K.

There are variations in the way psychiatric emergencies are being organised in different parts of the U.K. The most commonly practised model is described here.

FIGURE 4
Psychiatric emergency service in the U.K.

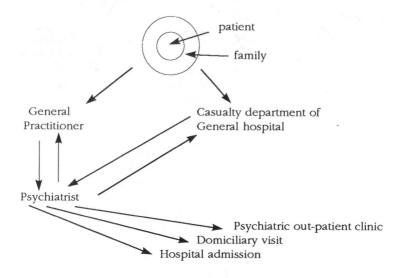

As outlined in Figure 4, psychiatric emergencies are either referred straight to the general practitioner or taken to the casualty department in a general hospital. The general practitioner would refer to the duty psychiatrist for the patient to be seen either in the psychiatric outpatient clinic or as a domiciliary visit. If the general practitioner feels that the emrgency cannot wait then he would ask the psychiatrist to admit the patient to the psychiatric ward immediately. If the patient is referred to casualty, the casualty officer again refers to the duty psychiatrist, who would arrange for the patient to be seen either in the casualty department, be followed up in the psychiatric outpatient clinic or be admitted to hospital. However, there are variations to this model.

Few districts in the U.K. practice the crisis intervention approach. Two well-known crisis intervention teams, Napsbury and Dingleton, provide a 24-hour, 7-day a week service. Napsbury crisis duty team includes a junior doctor, a psychiatric social worker and a psychiatric nurse. This team of three people would be involved 24-hours, 7-days a week throughout the year to deal with all crisis and psychiatric emergencies. No patient would be admitted without first going through this network. Coventry Crisis Intervention Team have a four-bedded house to provide social relief to people who are in distress and they also provide a domiciliary crisis service. This team is led by Social Services. Whilst some teams provide a 24-hour, 7-day a week crisis service, other teams provide only a daytime service because of limited resources, and also because of the difficulty in changing the subculture of psychiatric practice in the district.

FIGURE 5
Organisation of Huddersfield (west) Crisis Intervention Team

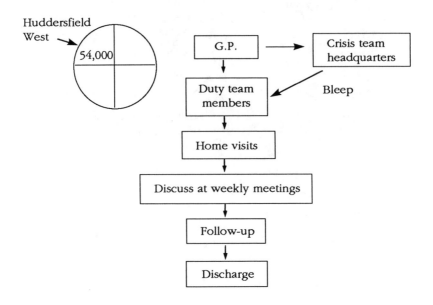

If a crisis occurs in the Huddersfield West area, there are two crisis therapists available to attend emergencies. Duty therapists are rotated daily; all therapists carry long-range bleeps for easy and rapid communication. The therapists will see the person and family in crisis in their own home and continue to follow-up and manage the crisis in that environment until discharge. The Management Plan and assessment are discussed regularly in team meetings, and the whole team provides support to keyworkers in the management of the crisis and in formulating the Management Plan.

Psychiatric emergency services in the U.S.A.

Psychiatric emergency services in the U.S.A. are organised in a totally different way to those in England. First of all, in the U.K. more than 90% of health services are provided by the National Health Service and are free to all, wheareas in America the majority of the service is provided by private psychiatric hospitals and clinics, with only a small part provided by the Government. In America, mental health workers do not normally see patients and families in crisis in their own homes. Patients in crisis are usually referred by the police and they are brought to the psychiatric emergency unit as outlined in Figure 6.

FIGURE 6

Psychiatric emergency service in the U.S.A.

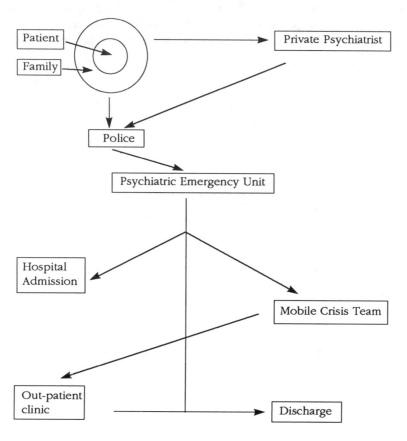

People who have private insurance may go to a private psychiatrist; if the psychiatrist finds that he cannot handle an emergency, then he would refer the case to the Emergency Psychiatric Unit situated in the district general hospital. The emergency psychiatric unit has a multi-disciplinary staff including psychiatrist, nurses, social workers, psychologists etc., and deals with initial assessment and immediate management. They may then refer people to a mental hospital for admission, or to a mobile crisis team or to an outpatient clinic. Because all of these teams are staffed by different personnel, the patient may have to relate to several psychiatrists and mental health professionals. These different teams tend to refer to each other depending on the progress of the patient. The disadvantage of this approach is that it lacks the continuity of the same team carrying through the treatment plan. There is a danger of the sensitive learning period being missed, so that it is too late for the mental health therapists to resolve the problems. Some teams do believe in the crisis model and apply crisis theory in the emergency psychiatric room within limitations, but in other emergency psychiatric units they practice using a traditional model with the main emphasis being on medical treatment. Both these approaches are carried out in clinics, rather than at the patient's own home.

FIGURE 7
Psychiatric emergency services in the USSR

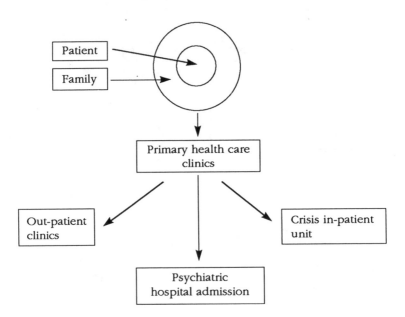

In the USSR, community mental health services are still not very well developed. A patient is referred to primary health care clinics and could be seen by either a primary health care doctor or a psychiatrist based at the clinic. From there, the patient could be referred to either a psychiatric outpatient clinic; for psychiatric hospital admission; or to a crisis inpatient unit. There is a separate ward for crisis inpatients in Moscow which deals exclusively with psychiatric emergencies from a wide area around Moscow. The treatment principles appear to be focused on a medical model. In the USSR some of the professions such as psychology, nursing, social work, occupational therapy, etc. are not fully evolved. Most of the mental health work is carried out by doctors, and a psychosocial approach is still in its early stages in the USSR.

FIGURE 8
Psychiatric emergency services in Australia

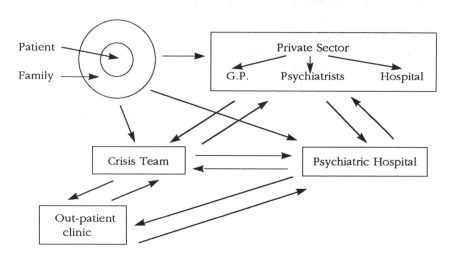

In Australia crisis intervention teams have developed rapidly throughout the country. More than 60% of New South Wales is covered by crisis teams, 24-hours a day, 7-days a week. They have been effective in reducing admission rates (Hoult, 1986), and in reducing the number of admission wards in psychiatric hospitals. As outlined in Figure 8, patients in Australia could be seen by a general practitioner or private psychiatrist and referred directly to the crisis team or a psychiatric hospital. Crisis teams maintain good contacts with psychiatric hospitals and tend to follow-up cases from the period of crisis until resolution.

Discussion

Organisation of crisis and psychiatric emergency services varies in different parts of the world, depending upon the different social, economic and political systems in those countries. Crisis teams are evolving in the community, but not all are really providing crisis service to people who are in psychiatric emergency. Some of them deal with only the "worried well", leaving the real emergencies to psychiatric hospital admission. In line with crisis concepts, patients in crisis should be seen in their own home; however, in some countries this is not possible, and crisis intervention principles are applied in outpatient clinics or in psychiatric emergency rooms. It is essential to involve the whole family during crisis. Not every home care treatment is based on the crisis model. In the U.K., traditional domiciliary visits by the psychiatrist and other professionals are assessed on a medical model. Good crisis teams differentiate between real crisis and furore. The intensive work is not useful to furore cases as they are not motivated to learn and change. Crisis intervention principles are also being applied increasingly in non-acute and chronic psychiatric practice but methods of treatment are different.

Concluding remarks

Crisis is a period of opportunity to learn new coping strategies to improve the individual's ability to cope with future crises without breaking down. Crisis intervention approaches differ between countries, depending upon their social, economic and political axial principles, and within the limitations and constraints put on mental health professionals. It has been found from research in various parts of the world that despite these difficulties, if the principles of crisis intervention are applied, crisis therapy would effectively deal with symptom remission, reduce hospital admissions and costs and provide better mental health care to people and families in crisis.

REFERENCES

CAPLAN, G. (1964) *Principles of Preventive Psychiatry* London: Tavistock Publications.

HOULT, J. (1986) Community Care of the Acutely Mentally Ill *British Journal of Psychiatry* 149:137-144.

ISHIKAWA, Y. (1991) Crisis Intervention and Treatment of Parent Abuse in Japan. In: N.R. Punukollu (ed.) *Recent Advances in Crisis Intervention, Vol. I* Huddersfield: International Institute of Crisis Intervention and Community Psychiatry Publications.

LANGSLEY, D.; KAPLAN, D.; PITTMAN, F.; MACHOTKA, P.; FLOMENHAFT, K. & DE YOUNG, C. (1968) *The Treatment of Families in Crisis* New York: Grune and Stratton.

LINDEMANN, E. (1944) Symptomatology and Management of Acute Grief *American Journal of Psychiatry* 101:141-148.

RATNA, L. (1978) *The Practice of Psychiatric Crisis Intervention* Napsbury: League of Friends.

STEIN, L.I. & TEST, M.A. (1980) Alternative to Mental Hospital Treatment: 1. Conceptual Model, Treatment Program and Clinical Evaluation *Archives of General Psychiatry* 37:392-397.

Family Crisis Intervention

Donald G. Langsley

This volume is concerned with crisis - a threat to the well-being of individuals and families. Crisis, as described by Shonkoff and his associates, imposes heavily on the basic organisation and structure of the family. Crisis tests a family's adaptive capacities and deficits in coping behaviour (combining trouble and opportunity); it also presents opportunity for growth.

The early work on the psychology of crisis focused on individuals. Using a homeostatic model, crisis was viewed in terms of external stress which precipitates an acutely uncomfortable state and regressive attempts to adapt, depending on the individual's strengths and old problems. Recent attention has been focused on the family either for its involvement in the crisis or as a resource for resolution of crisis. Earlier views suggested that the family precipitated or caused the crisis. A good example of this point of view is the outmoded concept of the schizophrenogenic mother. Later studies came to recognise that the family could be a resource in crisis management and that the family has always been the first resource in seeking help in a crisis. More recent views of the relationship between the family and crisis attend to prevention. Just as the family plays a role in precipitation of crisis or its management, the family can assist in both the primary and secondary prevention of a crisis. Using the concept of primary prevention, the family may offer strength in solving developmental problems so as to prevent a crisis. When an acute problem could become a crisis, early identification and intervention can prevent the development of more serious responses.

The past half century has added a series of social therapies and has extended the reasons for contact with others in the patient's social environment. Recognition of the psychopathologic features of the family structure of some patients led to the study of treatment for the whole family instead of the individual. This moved beyond the involvement of the family as a supplement or aid to individual therapy and into the realm of an ætiologic approach to psychopathology which involved the social system of the patient as well as the biologic and psychologic causes of psychiatric illness. Such an approach - which could be defined as treatment of the sick family rather than treatment of the sick individual - created a number of changes and complications. It became necessary to focus treatment on a group of people and to avoid labelling the one member of that family who had been the identified "patient".

Family studies initiated a period of rapid growth of interest in conjoint family therapy. By 1981 there were over 300 books published on family systems therapy, a dozen English language journals and two major professional associations of family therapists. Over 300 free-standing family therapy institutes had evolved in the USA. Gurman and Kniskern (1981) have categorised the schools of family psychology as being based on (1) psychoanalytic and object relations theory; (2) intergenerational; (3) based on systems theory; and (4) behavioural in orientation. In overviews of concepts of family functioning, Green and Hazelrigg (1981) point to basic processes:

1. The family is an open system.
2. It has stability as a role-governed system with a tendency towards stability and a capacity for change.
3. It uses processes of reciprocal influence with other human systems.
4. Families may develop communication disorders at multiple levels.
5. Individuals may precipitate family conflict resulting in efforts to submerge individuality in order to avoid family conflict.
6. Marital conflict and parental alliances influence family functioning.
7. Unresolved marital conflict gives rise to problems in the whole family.
8. When spouses can't resolve conflict, children may be triangled in to resolve the conflict.
9. Transference and projection processes create disturbed behaviour in either parents or children.
10. Involvement with families of origin influence the nuclear family.
11. There may be family rules about affect expression which result in anxious attachments.

My own interest in family crisis therapy began nearly thirty years ago when David Kaplan and I began working with families which included a member judged in need of immediate hospitalisation. By working with the whole family on a crisis-oriented basis we were able to demonstrate that such treatment could avoid the need for hospitalisation and the results of treatment were at least equivalent to those of hospital treatment. In 1968, when James Barter and I took responsibility for all mental health services in Sacramento County with a population of 700,000, we made major use of the techniques of family crisis therapy and drastically reduced the use of hospitals for the most seriously ill. Those experiments initiated a period of expanded use of family crisis therapy in many centres. In fact a recent literature search for papers on *family* crisis therapy identified almost a hundred journal articles published after 1980. One of the centres which has made use of family crisis techniques has been the outstanding programme at Madison, Winsconsin founded by Dr. Leonard Stein.

The life of the individual is so tied to the family that it is difficult to think about crisis management without a family orientation. To illustrate the family point of view one might examine the phenomenon of school refusal. A child afraid to go to school is often described as exhibiting behaviour representing an intrapsychic conflict. The school avoidance turns out to be a fear of separation from the mother instead of a phobia symbolizing an intrapsychic conflict. The clinical picture seems more one of separation anxiety but further study shows that the mother plays a part in this drama. The mother is ambivalent about the child's absence and communicates this in subtle interaction. To appreciate this the clinician must add an interactional element to the intrapsychic point of view. This dyadic view does not ignore the internal conflict, but adds another level of understanding which suggests that intervention might involve both the mother and child. If one looks beyond the dyad, it becomes clear that the relationship between the two is affected by problems in the relationship of father and mother. In viewing this added element, one moves to a family model. Behaviour is not determined entirely by psychological or biological forces, but is significantly influenced by the group and the social context in which it occurs. The family has a major impact on socialization and personality development, and in terms of symptom formation, the family point of view suggests that the conflicts which produce symptoms are not only intrapsychic, but also transactional. A dysfunctional family mismanages problems such as individuation, distance, closeness and separation in such a manner that social maturation is arrested. The problems do not cease with adolescence, but continue throughout adult life.

The family does not easily tolerate change and resists the movement which is required in therapy. The goals of family treatment are to improve the level of functioning and interaction so that no generation interferes with the individuation-separation of the adjacent generation. The therapist must help the family learn about itself as a transactional unit. The model of primary prevention suggests that helping families master certain points of hazard or developmental problems expected in any family can truly be viewed as prevention. Take for example, the normative transitions which are part of any family's development:

Marriage
Parenthood
School entry
Adolescence with its consequent separations
Adult crises such as unemployment or moving house
Marital crises with discord and separation or divorce
Crises associated with chronic illness or death.

An illustration of the possibility of avoiding crises associated with such transitions may be seen in the challenge of helping a child to learn. That carries with it an associated threat to a family where the mother is fearful of separation from the child. Berlin's (1975) work demonstrated the effect of early intervention on learning skills and the prevention of learning disorders. The work focused on mother-assisted learning at early stages of life. Working with children under age four, he was able to demonstrate improvement in vocabulary, reading, I.Q. and in concept learning. A similar project at Brookline, Massachusetts demonstrated that the most crucial times for learning skills are between eight and eighteen months. Early intervention and prevention in learning processes found improvement in the acquisition of learning skills. Studies in Florida (Gordon) and New York (Shaeffer) had similar findings.

A secondary prevention model focuses on early identification and intervention. This is more familiar to the clinician and calls for direct intervention. Crisis symptoms are viewed as the signal of stress (either external or internal) on the individual or family and inadequate coping results in regression and symptom formation in the susceptible population. When developmental crises, such as those cited above, are not mastered, the regression to previous (less effective or even pathologic) methods of problem solving often initiates a call for help from the family unable to resolve its own problems.

By working with the entire family in conjoint family crisis therapy, one

39

sees rapid improvement in the identified patient by virtue of the total family involvement. Conjoint family crisis therapy has been described for clarity as having several stages, but those are not really separate. The technique includes:

1. *Immediate aid.* Crisis therapy calls for rapid response since prolonging the problem will enhance the regression.
2. *Define the problem as within the family* (not just the individual). By seeing the family conjointly, the clinician places the locus of the problem in the total family. Treating one person only confirms the family's efforts to solve the problem by scapegoating.
3. *Focus on the present.* The current problem should be the focus of family crisis intervention. A detailed understanding of the past is not the major effort of this approach. Current events will help identify the precipitating crisis and will point to the family problem and thus to the steps needed to resolve it.
4. *Reduce the level of tension in the family.* Use any appropriate psychological and pharmacologic means. Immediate treatment and a hopeful attitude is reassuring. Medications should be made available for any member of the family requiring it, not just the identified patient.
5. *Help resolve the precipitating crisis* through negotiations about appropriate family roles or whatever active steps are necessary to aid the family to resolve the problem. By tension reduction and appropriate intervention, the family returns to its usual problem solving capacities and continues its development.
6. *Identify help for future crises.* Crisis therapy assumes that there will be future problems and the family should be given instructions about where to obtain aid in the future. Certain families or individual members of a family will also wish to be referred to sources of help for long term problems.

This approach to family crisis has been shown to avoid hospitalisation, even in the most seriously ill individuals. It results in reintegration of the regressed family member to the level of adaptation prior to the crisis and even results in demonstrable improvement of the family's ability to solve similar crises in the future. It is useful in walk-in clinics and emergency rooms. In primary care centres, other health professionals can be taught to use these techniques of family intervention. Jewett and associates (1982) demonstrated that paediatric residents could learn to manage family crises such as dealing with parents when the child has a potentially life-threatening illness. Evaluation of the instruction (one lecture and two parent crisis counselling instruction sessions) showed that skills acquired during even such brief instruction were useful in practice.

Wellish (1981) worked with families facing cancer where the major problem was learning to live with ambiguity in a group limited by their brutal fantasies about the future. Such families used family therapy on an "as needed" basis and the family therapist learned to deal with a series of crisis interactions. The locus of therapy was the family home, the therapist's office or the oncologist's office. The therapist enhanced the treatment of the medical problem by developing a coalition with the cancer treatment team or the primary oncologist. This helped avoid the splitting and mirroring of mistrust in the families. The treatment focused on education and modelling, attention to intimacy and boundaries, the effect of the cancer on the independence/dependence axis between patient and family and on attention to the management of frustration.

Kaufman (1985) has reviewed the research on the treatment of substance abuse by family therapy. The shift in family assessment for such problems has been from the nuclear family to a three generational system. There are separate studies on alcoholism and other drug abuse. Until recently the major interest was on the male alcoholic in his 40's and his over-involved spouse. However, families where a parent is an alcoholic apparently produce drug abusing and alcoholic children. In the treatment of families which include an alcoholic the most fruitful approach has been on marital interactional dynamics, role perceptions and marital patterns of expectations and sanctions about alcohol. Based on clinical reports, Kaufman is encouraged about the usefulness of family therapy for this problem, and even more impressed with the usefulness of family therapy for drug abuse.

A nursing team has reported on family crisis intervention in the medical intensive care unit (Hodovanic, 1984). They report that the family's response to the illness may affect the outcome for the individual. The family is confronted with role changes, isolation from the ill member, financial concerns and fear of loss. Needs identified include the need for hope, the need to relive the critical incident, the fear of criticizing hospital staff and the need for medical information. An initial assessment and active efforts to contact the family were part of the therapy. It included a daily phone call from the nurse to at least one member of the family. Educational efforts about the treatment and the frightening equipment being used aided the family to master their fears. A follow-through effort, even when the patient died, permitted families to master this outcome.

Another group who benefit from family therapy are hospitalised psychiatric patients. Lansky (1981) points out that general psychiatry, especially hospital psychiatry, has become increasingly biologic. Practice tends to ignore psychosocial factors, especially the family. Many patients who would profit from family therapy do not get it, and this is detrimental to the overall effectiveness of treatment, according to Lansky. He calls for a new eclecticism to overcome specific target symptoms in the psychopathology, deal with problems of *family* psychopathology and with problems of medication discontinuance. In doing family therapy with hospitalised patients, it is necessary to be aware of the effects of the hospital as a containment factor. Splitting ocurs when the hospital fails to anticipate the family sensitivity to blame or when management issues are settled outside the family sessions.

Goldstein (in Lanksy, 1981) has reported on crisis-oriented six-session family therapy for families which include a schizophrenic to help the family accept that the patient is psychotic, to help the family identify some of the precipitating stresses, and to identify future stress to which the patient and family are likely to be vulnerable. Patients were rated on success in achieving

41

these objectives and on psychopathology. The impact of family therapy on blunted affect was that those who received it showed less residual psychopathology than no-therapy cases (measured on the BPRS) and that the sustained effect of high dose plus therapy group persisted long after patients were in therapy. Both phenothiazines and family therapy played a significant role in decreasing relapse in acute young schizophrenics after discharge. The patients who were on higher doses were more likely to stay on medication if they had family therapy. Those who were rated as achieving the objectives of family therapy continued to show decreases in thought disorder. Goldstein concluded that crisis oriented family therapy added significantly to the results of the drug therapy.

Family therapy was studied as an adjunct to inpatient therapy in Glick's Payne-Whitney study as well as the Goldstein study. It was used to supplement standard inpatient treatment. Using a true experimental model, patients were randomly assigned to family therapy plus individual therapy or just individual therapy. The final report on 186 patients included groups of (1) schizophrenics with good pre-hospital functioning for 18 months prior to admission; (2) schizophrenics with poor pre-hospital functioning; (3) major affective disorders; and (4) other Axis I disorders. The inpatient family intervention improved the outcome of the female patients with affective disorders and improved attitudes toward treatment in the families of patients with either affective disorders or schizophrenia.

The Langsley-Kaplan study done in Denver from 1964-69 tested the effect of outpatient crisis family therapy for patients who would ordinarily have been hospitalised. A group of 150 families in the experimental group were compared with another group of 150 families where the identified patient was hospitalised. Random assignment to treatment, baseline evaluation and multiple outcome measures including independent assessment at 6, 18 and 30 months after discharge were used. In all 150 cases treated with family therapy, it was possible to avoid hospitalisation. On measures of role functioning and symptoms, the family therapy cases did as well as the hospitalised patients; and on measures of crisis resolution and time before return to functioning, the family therapy cases did better than the hospitalised cases. The Denver programme was the basis for further comparisons done in the Sacramento Mental Health programme where an experimental design was not used, but it was the conclusion of those in the programme that crisis family therapy was a useful alternative to hospital admission.

Crisis intervention for crises involving adolescents is the subject of a report by Gutstein and colleagues (1988). He calls his method for mobilizing families and networks a System Crisis Intervention Program (SCIP). A crisis occurs when kinship systems have reached a point of crisis overload. He uses a variety of temporary emergency responses including 24 hour hospitalisation, daily outpatient visits, partial hospitalisation, emergency shelter and medications. In a study with this population, he accepted referrals only when there was a clear recommendation for psychiatric hospital admission, evidence of the recent precipitation of some type of self-destructive crisis behaviour and a family which was disturbed by the behaviour. His treatment techniques included seeing the family within 24 hours of a call. Treatment consisted of one three-hour evaluation, 6-10 one-hour preparation sessions with individual family members and two four-hour extended family gatherings. Common problems were suicidal behaviour, severe depression, violent behaviour, drug abuse and chronic school refusal. The study showed effectivenes of his crisis intervention in resolving the crisis behaviour. Of 75 patients, only 5 had to be hospitalised. His measures showed significant improvement from baseline by three months, and further improvement at six and 24 months.

Family therapy also has a role in delinquency. Tolan (1986) summarised a number of studies which reveal that families of delinquents may be distinguishable from other families by their interactional sequences and processes. The treatment approaches receiving the most support are behavioural, structural, strategic and communication. There has been increased scepticism about treatment or rehabilitation for delinquency, but family focused interventions have gained support. In 31 studies summarised, the most useful are those with clear conceptualisation about family functioning, delinquency patterns and family therapy.

There is considerable evidence that family therapies of several types (including family crisis therapy) are at least as effective as individual psychotherapy for problems which focus on marital or family conflict. Family therapies are often *more* effective than individual treatment, even for some problems which do not present as interpersonal. Structural family therapy has had encouraging support for treatment of childhood and adolescent psychosomatic symptoms such as anorexia and asthma. Gurman and Kniskern (1981) suggest that it should be seen as the treatment of choice for childhood psychosomatic conditions. Additionally, structural family therapy with drug addicts is reported to have some of the best controlled outcome studies in the research literature on family therapy. Behavioural family therapy has had interesting outcomes in the treatment of adolescents involved in "soft" juvenile delinquency. We are pleased to see family therapy, especially family crisis therapy, extended, tested, and found useful over these past thirty years.

REFERENCES

Berlin, I.N. (ed.) (1975) *Advocacy for Child Mental Health* New York: Brunner-Mazel.

Green R.J. (1981) An Overview of Major Contributions to Family Therapy. In: R.J. Green and J.L. Framo (eds.) *Family Therapy: Major Contributions* New York: International University Press.

Goldstein, M.J. (1981) Family Therapy During the Aftercare Therapy of Acute Schizophrenia. In: M.R. Lansky (ed.) *Family Therapy and Major Psychopathology* New York: Grune & Stratton.

GURMAN, A.S. & KNISKERN, D.P. (1981) Family Therapy Outcome Research: Knowns and Unknowns. In: A.S. Gurman & D.P. Kniskern (eds.) *Handbook of Family Therapy* New York: Brunner-Mazel.

GUTSTEIN, S.E.; RUDD M.D.; GRAHAM, J.C. & RAYHA, L.L. (1988) Systemic Crisis Intervention as a Response to Adolescent Crises: An Outcome Study *Family Process* **27**:201-211.

HAZELRIGG, M.D.; COOPER, H.M. & BORDUIM, C.M. (1987) Evaluating the Effectiveness of Family Therapy: An Integrated Review and Analysis. *Psychological Bulletin* **101**:428-442.

HODOVANIC, B.H;, REARDON, D.; REESE, W. & HEDGES, B. (1984) Family Crisis Intervention Program in the Medical Intensive Care Unit *Heart and Lung* **13**:243-249.

JEWETT, L.S.; GREENBERG, L.W.; CHAMPION, L.A.A.; GLUCK, R.S.; LEIKIN, S.L.; ALTIERI, M.F. & LIPNICK, R.N. (1982) Teaching of Crisis Counselling Skills to Paediatric Residents: A One Year Study *Paediatrics* **70**:907-911.

KAUFMAN, E. (1985) Family Systems and Family Therapy of Substance Abuse: An Overview of Two Decades of Research and Clinical Experience *International Journal of Addictions* **20**:897-916.

LANGSLEY, D.G.; MACHOTKA, P. & FLOMENHAFT, K. (1971) Avoiding Mental Hospitalisation: A Follow-Up Study *American Journal of Psychiatry* **127**:1391-1394.

LANSKY, M.R. (ed.) (1981) *Family Therapy and Major Psychopathology* New York: Grune & Stratton.

SPENCER, J.H.; GLICK, I.D.; HAAS, G.L.; CLARKIN, J.F.; LEWIS, A.B.; PEYSER, J.; DEMARE, N.; GOOD-ELLIS, M.; HARRIS, E. & LESTELLE, V. (1988) A Randomized Clinical Trial of Inpatient Family Interventions. III: Effects at 6 Month and 18 Month Follow-Ups *American Journal of Psychiatry* **145**:1115-1121.

STEIN, L.E. & TEST, M.A. (eds.) (1978) *Alternatives to Mental Hospital Treatment* New York: Plenum Press.

TOLAN, P.H.; CROMWELL, R.E. & BRASSWELL, M. (1986) Family Therapy with Delinquents: A Critical Review of the Literature *Family Process* **25**:619-649.

WELLISCH, D.K. (1981) Helping Disturbed Families Cope with Cancer. In: M.R. Lansky (ed.) *Family Therapy and Major Psychopathology* New York: Grune & Stratton.

Management of Acute Psychiatric Problems in the Community with Crisis

John Hoult

Querido in Amsterdam, prior to the Second World War, developed the first crisis teams - mobile teams which visited new patients in their homes. The next development in the care of the mentally ill occurred in Britain after the War; wards were unlocked, short admissions came into vogue. By the 1960's, operating out of Dingleton Hospital in Scotland and Napsbury Hospital in England, mobile psychiatric teams visited patients in their own homes and if possible treated them there. Crisis teams had come to Britain. Also in the 1960's, similar developments were going on in the USA. Pasamanick in Kentucky, Langsley in Denver, and later Pollack in Denver and Stein in Wisconsin developed their ideas about how acutely mentally ill people could be treated in the community as an alternative to hospital admission.

Some of these programmes have been well researched, and I would refer you to a review article by Braun and his colleagues (1981) for further information on this. Research in this area is important because it gives the approach credibility. The best research is that done by Dr. Len Stein and his colleague Mary Ann Test; it has the best methodology, it has the fewest exclusions among its subjects and it has a long follow-up. Not only that, Stein and Test had the most comprehensive programme of treatment. It was the Stein and Test work that was the model on which we based our own work in Sydney.

In the 1970's in Sydney, the system of care we call Community Care was not really an effective way of doing things. When patients came out of hospital there were few staff to help them; most of the community mental health workers had found their clientele among basically healthy people, helping them solve problems of relationships. Some claimed to be doing primary preventions, helping to stop people developing schizophrenia or manic-depressive illness, although there is no evidence that we can actually prevent such illnesses. Those with established mental illness were neglected.

As a step to developing a comprehensive system of care to deal with the mentally ill, in 1979 we decided in Sydney to replicate the study of Stein and Test. This research has been published in detail elsewhere, so I will just give a brief summary here.

In New South Wales, any medical practitioner can write a medical certificate stating that a person is mentally ill, and that certificate is all that is needed for a patient to be brought compulsorily to hospital, if necessary with police assistance. At the front door of the hospital, they are seen by the doctor on duty (usually a junior doctor) who decides whether or not to admit the person. In our study, we randomly allocated patients who came to Macquarie (Mental) Hospital for admission. The control group were dealt with according to usual procedures, i.e. most were admitted, stayed in hospital several weeks until their symptoms and behaviour settled and were then discharged for follow-up care to one of the six community mental health centres in the area. The experimental group patients were managed by a special team which did not admit them if possible, but rather took them to the patient's own home or to other community settings and treated them there. All patients were followed up in the research for 12 months from date of entry.

TABLE 1
Number of admissions to psychiatric hospitals or clinics during 12 months study period*

	Experimental (n=53)	Control (n=47)
None	32 (60%)	2 (4%)
1	17 (32%)	21 (45%)
2	2 (4%)	17 (36%)
3	1 (2%)	5 (11%)
4+	1 (2%)	2 (4%)

John Hoult "Community Care of the Acutely Mentally Ill", *British Journal of Psychiatry* **149**:137-144 (1986), Table 1. (Reprinted with permission of the British Journal of Psychiatry

As you can see from Table 1, there was quite a significant difference in the number of admissions in each group. Most of the control group were admitted to hospital, and about half the group were re-admitted in the 12 months follow-up period. (This is a common finding around the world; between 30% and 50% of patients who are discharged from psychiatric units are re-admitted within 12 months.) On the other hand, only 40% of the experimental group were admitted during the twelve month period, and very few were re-admitted in that year.

TABLE 2
Length of stay in psychiatric hospitals or clinics during 12 months study period*

	Experimental (n=53)	Control (n=47)
Not admitted	32 (60%)	2 (4%)
Less than 1 week	14 (26%)	11 (23%)
1-2 weeks	0 (0%)	6 (13%)

(cont.)

	Experimental (n=53)	Control (n=47)
3-4 weeks	3 (6%)	5 (11%)
5-6 weeks	3 (6%)	8 (17%)
7-10 weeks	0 (0%)	4 (9%)
11-15 weeks	0 (0%)	6 (13%)
16 weeks or more	1 (2%)	5 (10%)

*John Hoult *op.cit.* Table II. (Reprinted with permission of the British Journal of Psychiatry)

The average length of stay was quite short for our group compared to the control group, so our reason for fewer admissions was not longer length of stay.

The experimental group had lower scores on the Present State Examination at the end of the follow-up period, i.e. they were less symptomatic than the control group, though both groups had started the study with similar symptom levels. The level of functioning for both groups showed no statistically significant difference at 12 months; comparison of the different measures of functioning did show trends in favour of the experimental group, but these did not reach statistical significance.

TABLE 3
Mean Present State Examination total and sub-scores at baseline and 12 months*

	Baseline			Twelve months		
	Experimental (n=58)	Control (n=57)	Sig	Experimental (n=52)	Control (n=46)	SIg
Mean total PSE score	30.5	30.9	NS	9.8	15.4	P<0.001
Mean DAH (delusional and hallucinatory syndromes)	8.2	8.4	NS	1.9	4.0	P<0.001
Mean BSO (behaviour, speech and other syndromes)	7.0	7.3	NS	2.0	3.1	P<0.001
Mean SNR (specific neurotic syndromes)	4.5	5.0	P<0.01	1.4	2.4	P<0.001
Mean NSN (non-specific neurotic syndromes)	10.5	11.6	P<0.01	4.2	6.0	P<0.001

* John Hoult *op.cit.* Table III. (Reprinted with permission of the British Journal of Psychiatry.)

The next table shows that patients and their relatives preferred the experimental treatment to the usual method of treatment. The patient's responses were anticipated - most patients do not like hospital - but not the relatives' responses. Clearly, if we had transferred a burden of care to the relatives, they did not find it less preferable to what they had previously experienced.

TABLE 4

Summary of patients' and relatives' satisfaction with care received during the 12 months study period[1]

	Control[2] %	Experimental[2] %	Sig
Patients very satisfied with advice and information	29	60	P<0.01
Patients very satisfied with support and help	33	65	P<0.01
Patients very satisfied with amount of supervision	12	56	P<0.001
Patients preferring admission to community treatment	25	12	NS
Relatives very satisfied with support and help patients received	28	83	P<0.001
Relatives very satisfied with the amount of supervision patients received	30	85	P<0.001
Relatives who themselves received enough support and information	39	88	P<0.001
Relatives coping better during study year than before	28	70	P<0.001
Relatives preferring hospital admission to community treatment	35	2	P<0.01

[1] John Hoult *op.cit.* Table IV. (Reprinted with permission of the British Journal of Psychiatry.)

[2] *The numbers were 53 experimental and 48 control patients and 48 experimental and 47 control relatives.*

Health economists costed the average amount of money required for patients in each groups. The experimental group treatment cost Aus $4489 for the year for each patient; the control group cost was $5669 per patient per annum (costs are in 1979 dollars). The experimental group treatment cost 26% less and returned a better outcome.

We did not want this project to be just a demonstration, with no subsequent development, so we have worked on our bureaucrats and our politicians to accept the principles of care used in our study as the basis for further developments of community services. Fortuitously, in 1982 the State Government held an inquiry into mental health services. We addressed the inquiry, using our research (and that of others) as the support for our recommendations. The inquiry accepted much of what we told it, and in its own recommendations said that a comprehensive range of community based services should be set up, including a mobile, 24-hour crisis team in each health area. Because these new services were to be funded by transfer of money from the mental hospitals, there was a great deal of opposition from staff in the mental hospitals, and from the health unions. Nevertheless, the Government went ahead and began setting up these services, health area by health area throughout the State. In 1988, in the State election, the Labour Party Government was replaced by the Liberal Party (the equivalent of the British Conservative Party) which had campaigned vigorously against the run-down of the mental hospitals. Once in power, however, they have continued the policy of the previous government under a slightly different guise.

New South Wales has a population of 5.6 million, only slightly larger than that of Scotland. Currently, we have crisis teams covering about 60% of the population, and by the end of 1991 we anticipate about 90% of the population will have such coverage. Some teams are very good, some are not so good, i.e. not so responsive, not so energetic, not so careful in their monitoring of the emergency situation. It takes more than just providing sufficient staff to ensure a good service. Other Australian States are following a similar path. Victoria now has five crisis teams, and Western Australia has recently developed its first one (see Michael Ash, this volume).

There are of course, developments in crisis services going on in Britain. I visited Dr. Punukollu's team in Huddersfield in 1990, and have previously seen the one in Birmingham run by Dr. Christine Dean. These are excellent services. The Napsbury one continues, and the work of others is reflected in this and the following volumes. In the United States, mobile crisis teams are developing too. I think, however, it is much easier for us in the British Commonwealth to get good effective crisis services going than it is in the United States, because of the incredibly chaotic and archaic system of health care in that country. With regard to developments in the rest of the world, I know little, but hope to learn from my fellow contributors.

I want to make a very important point. A crisis service is not something which should stand alone. It should be just one part of a network of services for the mentally ill. Figure 1 overleaf demonstrates my point.

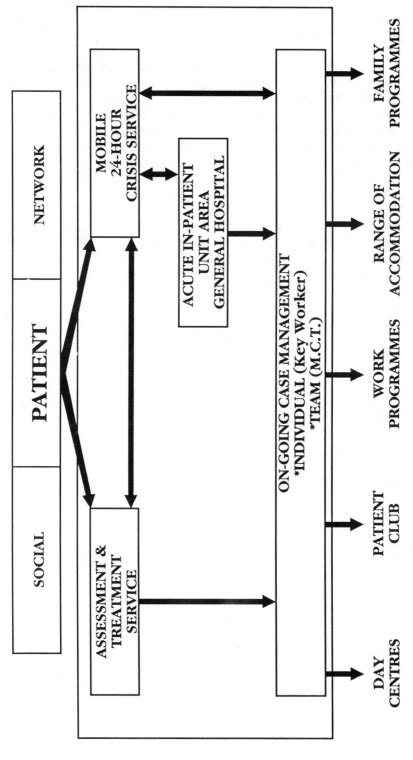

FIGURE 1: Relationship of crisis services to network of services for the mentally ill

The patient is of course, part of a social network, and I have shown it here. He enters the service either routinely via the assessment and treatment service, based in the community mental health centre or in the outpatient department, or in an emergency via the 24-hour mobile crisis service. If the patient's problems or behaviour are more than the assessment and treatment service can reasonably manage, the crisis service is asked to assist until they resolve it. If things are more difficult than even this team can handle, then the patient will require admission to the area's general hospital psychiatric unit. However, the crisis service is the gate-keeper to the in-patient unit; that is important. Where this does not happen, we can sometimes find the crisis service becomes underutilised, especially if the in-patient unit is not part of the overall service and for whatever reason needs to keep its beds occupied. Having a crisis team allows earlier discharge for patients from in-patient care. The crisis team can visit several times daily to monitor progress and supervise treatment.

Once the acute phase of the ilness has subsided, most patients will need on-going care. They will need a case manager (or as you say in Britain, a key worker), a staff person who accepts responsibility for overseeing that patient's care, making sure that what needs to be done gets done and that the patient stays in care. Some patients are very difficult to manage; they are demanding, or very non-compliant, or simply require enormous effort to ensure that even their basic needs are met. Such patients are best managed not individually but by a team. Dr. Stein and his colleagues set up the first such team in Madison, Wisconsin, and now the concept is spreading across the USA and to Australia. In these teams, the staff to patient ratio is about 1 to 10, quite high, but the result is that the most difficult patients are not neglected; their needs are attended to, they receive regular medication, their condition stabilises, and over a period of a year or two they can improve considerably. The team approach helps share the burden for the staff, and patients form a good relationship with the team. We have three such teams in Sydney, and I have visited quite a number of similar teams in the USA; all of them are helping to stabilise patients who previously were thought to be beyond help.

Of course, there is more to helping people than just case management. The diagram on the previous page refers to just some of a large variety of services which a mentally ill person might need, and which a good area service will need to provide. The case managers help the patient access such services. Recently I was in Cambridge and saw a most impressive array of rehabilitation facilities and services organised under the direction of Dr. Geoff Shepherd. Let me draw your attention to another important aspect of the care of the mentally ill, viz. the family. They need explanation, guidance, support and in return we have found them to be quite willing to support our services and to lobby the administrators and politicians on our behalf.

To repeat, a crisis service is not the only component of a good, comprehensive service for the mentally ill. On the other hand, you cannot have a good service without one.

The organisation of crisis services in New South Wales is usually a multi-disciplinary team of nurses, social workers and psychologists. The teams work seven days a week, two shifts a day. We like to have at least three staff on the morning shift and two on the evening shift. Having just one person on for a shift means either that patients settling down cannot be attended to, or a new patient cannot be helped. However, from 11pm till 8am we have one staff at home on call with a long range pager. This person is not usually called out. There is also 24-hour medical cover (both registrar and consultant) in metropolitan areas.

The key to our service is that it is mobile, able to respond rapidly, able to spend a lot of time with patients and relatives, and makes a priority to link the patient with on-going care.

What do the staff working on crisis teams actually do when they deal with a psychiatric patient in some kind of emergency? Well, the answer is nothing sophisticated, just good common sense. Granted that common sense is not very common, it is still something that most staff can learn quickly enough. Basically, a crisis team assesses, plans, implements and evaluates. These four phases are not distinct in practice; during the assessment phase treatment can commence, and vice versa. Assessment and planning begin with the referral phone call: How urgent should the response be? Should one or two people make the initial assessment? Should a doctor accompany them? Is there likely to be danger?

Our initial assessments are usually made in the person's home. The first task is to assess what is the presenting problem, and who has it. Often it is not the identified patient who has the presenting problem - he says he has no problem at all! - it is the relatives or a policeman. Failure to identify the problem and its owner can clearly lead to problems further along if we attempt to deal with what we think is the problem but others do not share our perception. Relatives may identify the patient's problem as delusions or hallucinations, but in fact almost always it is some kind of behavioural disturbance, such as threatening harm to themselves or others, or not caring for themselves, or being disorganised or noisy.

Other factors to be assessed include clinical symptoms and signs, i.e. the presence or absence of disorders of thought, mood, behaviour and perception. Special attention must be given to disorders of behaviour, because these are the ones which will determine whether or not the patient can be managed outside hospital; unsafe or intolerable behaviour will make our task a lot more difficult. The quality of the person's social relationships also have to be assessed: are they supportive or are they harmful? This also determines where the patient will be managed; it may be more appropriate that the patient moves to other accommodation if there is major friction. Also needing to be assessed are the physical resources the patient can call on - things like money, clothing, food, shelter. Some must be addressed immediately, others in the next day or so. Finally, we have to assess the patient's willingness to co-operate with us; if he refuses, we have to decide whether to accept his refusal or to take him compulsorily to hospital. Not infrequently, co-operation is given grudgingly and we have to focus on building a relationship as quickly as possible. These then are the things we need to assess. This assessment requires much more intensive input outside hospital; with in-patients it can be done over several days at the staff's leisure.

The next phase is planning. A crisis team must involve the patient and relatives in this phase not only to ensure their co-operation in the final plan, but also to gain the benefits of their knowledge and wisdom. Often we will propose a wide range of options - even quite extreme ones - to them, to let them know we are willing to consider all possibilities. We make sure they know the plan is not static, and will be changed as events develop. As we work on the plan, we convey to the patient the expectation that he is going to have to behave himself; even if he has ben causing mayhem up till now, from now on he is going to have to behave properly.

By the implementation phase, we have usually spent quite a bit of time talking to the patient and his relatives. Right back in 1979, in the days of our original research, we discovered how important it was to spend time talking. We can see a patient initially and think that there is no way we can do anything but hospitalise that patient, his behaviour is so disturbed; after an hour or so an alternative course of action suggests itself as a possibility, and after two hours we wonder what on earth made us think this person needed to be in hospital. Of course what is also happening during this time is that we are forming quite a relationship with the patient.

Implementing the agreed treatment plan usually means a lot of visiting. In the beginning, we err on the side of over-visiting, in order to reassure the patient and family that we mean what we say, that we are available to them at short notice and we want to make sure everything will settle down well. This gives everyone a great sense of security, ensures any deterioration is quickly detected, and furthers the building of the relationship between patient, relatives and the team.

This latter point is, I think, one of the major differences between crisis teams and more traditional services: crisis teams become almost part of the family system and retain the right of easy entry into that system.

What else happens in implementation? We explain to everyone what we think has happened. We give advice and guidance. We are quite directive, telling the patient and relatives what should and should not be done, what behaviour is not tolerable. Of course there is give and take in this, and mostly it is not as blunt as I am making it sound. The point is we do not shrink from being directive. We do a lot of supervision. We may call several times a day to make sure medication is being swallowed. We make sure patients go for blood tests, for GP and dental and other appointments. We may work with them to help them tidy up their flat, or get rid of the cockroaches, or whatever else is needed to be done to improve their reasonable quality of life. Counselling also takes place in this phase.

An interesting consequence happens if relatives feel supported. If they know they can reach you at any hour of the night, they usually do not call you. Naturally there will be one or two notorious exceptions, but most will persevere with the patient because they know if things really get too bad they can call and get you, but since you have been so good to them they would rather not disturb your sleep.

During the implementation phase relatives learn a lot by watching us deal with the patient. They learn - as best as we can teach them - the difference between bad and mad, and how to deal with each. They can accept the necessity of letting go of the patient, feeling reasonably confident that we will be supervising him, and will be reporting back to them on his progress.

As I mentioned, plans are not immutable, and sadly implementation of the plans often does not go the way it should. In the evaluation phase, the results of the process of implementation are examined and new plans made - in conjunction once again with patient and relatives.

Table 5 lists the principles of care we think are important for crisis teams. Most of them are self-explanatory, but I would like to address the issue of assertive care. I believe we have to have an assertive approach, otherwise our efforts will be ineffective in many cases, hospital admission will be the ultimate result and patient and relatives will have suffered doubly. The analogy is with a door to door salesman: ultimately the patient has the right to say no, but we are entitled to try as hard as we can to convince him of the advantages of our treatment. Even if they do reject us, we will go to the relatives or other significant person, explain what we would like to do and that we have been rebuffed, and indicate our willingness to get re-involved as soon as the status quo changes. Some health workers see this assertiveness as infringing patients rights to privacy. I do not agree; we accept their right to finally say no, but we are only too aware that their refusal will often lead to even greater infringements of their rights via compulsory admission and treatment.

TABLE 5
Principles of care for crisis teams

- Intensive in the beginning
- Mobile
- Accessible in time and place
- Responsive
- Flexible
- Assertive
- Deals with problems in-vivo
- Includes social network
- Ensures link to on-going care

Finally, I would like to give you some of the reasons why I think there are advantages to not admitting patients into hospital. In Britain, quite a number of psychiatrists have asked what is wrong with a short admission? Why strive so hard to avoid it? I shall enumerate some reasons.

1. *Stigma*: In the common view, a mental patient is someone who has been in a mental hospital. Stigma attaches to psychiatric units in general hospitals too.

2. *Patients and relatives prefer it*: In Dr. Stein' study, in our own original study, and in our latest study of a routine service in the Ryde/Hunter's Hill area of Sydney, the results have consistently shown that community treatment is overwhelmingly preferred by both experimental and control groups.

3. *Community treatment demystifies the illness for the patient and relatives:* They tend to think that mental illness is something mysterious going on inside a black box inside the patient, and only the doctors have a key to that box. The doctors take the patient away to hospital, do something magical there and the patient comes back a little better, though not cured. When patients are with our crisis teams, we do a lot of explaining about what is going on, and even more importantly, by demonstrating in front of relatives what needs to be done, we take away the mystery.

4. *Community treatment helps prevent patients taking on the sick role:* Because we put expectations on them to lead as normal a life as possible. It also helps prevent patients taking on the identity of a mental patient. Many of you will be familiar with "The Treatment Barrier", an important paper by Dr. Dennis Scott of Napsbury Hospital, written some 17 years ago.

5. *Community care teaches the patient and relatives the difference between mad and bad*: In traditional care, this rarely happens, but crisis teams are forced to explain that symptoms such as hallucinations are part of the illness and will respond to medication in most cases, but abusive behaviour is usually not directly a part of the illness and needs to be dealt with quite differently. Relatives watch us deal with this behaviour in a quite firm way, and the patients knows his relatives are watching us and learning.

6. *Patient, staff and relatives are forced in community care to develop a relationship*: In traditional care, patients and relatives complain they do not get to see a constant therapist often enough; with our crisis teams this does not happen. We have to see the patient and relatives quite often in order to monitor progress and develop short and long term plans. In Sydney, a useful device called "Laser Therapy" has emerged. (The Area Health Authorities provide cars for use by crisis teams and the make of car most often provided is one made by the Ford Motor Company called a Laser!) A crisis team member often takes one of our more acute patients with him or her in the Laser visiting other patients. This does a lot of things. It gives the patient and

relatives a break from each other, the patient gets a new environment with constantly changing scenery, the staff person monitors the patient's behaviour, but most importantly the staff person and the patient have to talk to each other, to make ordinary conversation about the weather, the traffic, television, whatever. The relationship that develops is an important therapeutic tool.

To conclude, research has shown that crisis teams can be effective in the care of the mentally ill. Patients and relatives express their preference for them. A crisis team or service must be mobile, and offer extensive, preferably 24-hour cover. It is an important component of a comprehensive network of community-based services for the mentally ill, and should have as one of its major goals the engagement of the patient and relatives in on-going care.

REFERENCES

BRAUN, P.; KOCHANSKY, G.; SHAPIRO, R.; GREENBERG, S.; GUDEMAN, J.E.; JOHNSON, S. & SHORE, M.F. (1981) Overview; Desinstitutionalisation of Psychiatric Patients: A Critical Review of Outcome Studies *American Journal of Psychiatry* **136**:736-749.

Department of Health, New South Wales (1983) *Psychiatric Hospital Versus Community Treatment - A Controlled Study* Sydney: Department of Health, New South Wales.

HOULT, J. (1986) Community Care of the Acutely Mentally Ill *British Journal of Psychiatry* **149**:137-144.

HOULT, J.; REYNOLDS, I.; CHARBONNDAN-POWIS, M.; WEEKES, R. & BRIGGS, J. (1983) Psychiatric Hospital versus Community Treatment: The Results of a Randomised Trial *Australian & New Zealand Journal of Psychiatry* **17**:160-169.

LANGSLEY, D.G. & KAPLAN, D.M. (1968) *The Treatment of Families in Crisis* New York: Grune & Stratton.

PASAMANICK, B. (1964) Home Versus Hospital Care for Schizophrenics *Journal of the American Medical Association* **187**:177-181.

POLAK, P.R. & KIRBY, M.W. (1976) A Model to Replace Psychiatric Hospitals *Journal of Nervous and Mental Diseases* **162**:13-21.

REYNOLDS, I. & HOULT, J. (1984) The Relatives of the Mentally Ill: A Comparative Trial of Community-Oriented and Hospital-Oriented Care *Journal of Nervous and Mental Disease* **172**:480-489.

REYNOLDS, I.; JONES, J.; BERRY, D. & HOULT, J. (1990) A Crisis Team for the
Mentally Ill: The Effect on Patients, Relatives and Admissions *Medical Journal
of Australia* **152**:646-652.

SCOTT, R.D. (1973) The Treatment Barrier *British Journal of Medical Psychology*
46:45-67.

STEIN, L.I. & TEST, M.A. (1980) Alternative to Mental Hospital Treatment: I.
Conceptual Model, Treatment Program and Clinical Evaluation *Archives of
General Psychiatry* **37**:392-397.

Crisis Intervention Where it is Contraindicated

Lawrence Ratna

If it is the exception that proves the rule, then it is the contraindication that is perhaps the most sensitive measure of the functional capacity of a crisis service. In this paper I want to explore the limits of crisis intervention: what are its contraindications, and what can be done about them? In short, to foolishly rush in where crisis interveners are reluctant to tread!

The commonest contraindication by far is mental illness. Many services do not consider crisis intervention appropriate if the client is mentally ill. This raises a central question. What is a crisis and what is a mental illness? The general answer seems to be a developmental one. Crisis is a stage in the evolution of a mental illness - i.e. if the crisis is not resolved the tension mounts and the client deteriorates into mental illness. This is the raison d'être for many crisis programmes - by intervening early at the stage of crisis the descent into madness is arrested. The consequence of this is that if the patient is already mentally ill at referral then it is too late for crisis intervention and it is dealt with on conventional lines.

The services that use mental illness as an excluding criterion tend to take on the kind of patients that are regarded as suitable for psychotherapy, the differences being that the former take clients on more quickly, are more directive and are brief in their interventions. These services tend to be operated by psychologists, social workers, counsellors (i.e. non-medical professionals) and are generally more common in the United States. They tend to function as a separate service running parallel to conventional psychiatric programmes, screening their clients carefully.

The mirror images of these services are the comprehensive services which do not screen patients except perhaps by catchment area. They define crisis not in terms of psychopathology or in terms of suitability for treatment but purely in terms of urgency of demand. For them a crisis is an urgent demand for immediate psychiatric treatment. This fits the concept of a medical emergency rather than a Caplanian conflict with an unresolved problem.

Between these two extremes lie services that use a mixture of these models and the question "What is a crisis and who defines it?" is fundamental to practice but unresolved in theory.

If one reviews the literature, however, one can find certain client categories that crisis interveners all over the world like to avoid.

These are: the elderly; violent patients; the suicidal; the psychotic; drug addicts; chronic patients.

Let me narrow the field down. One man's beef is another man's BSE; what one service considers a contraindication is often a prime indication for another. The suicidal are a key case in point. Many crisis programmes, particularly of the parallel type, exclude them. On the other hand the suicidal are, by and large, the population most commonly dealt with by crisis programmes. These tend to be specialised for suicide prevention, tend to work closely with medical services in emergency rooms and have access to psychiatric beds for involuntary care. The polar opposite of that would be telephone counselling services that seek to befriend and counsel the suicidal, for example, the Samaritans. Truly, the services for the suicidal are as varied as the means we have to kill ourselves.

The reader must look elsewhere in this and the following volumes for work carried out within a crisis intervention framework with (a) violent and (b) chronic patient groups. The psychotic are a relative crisis. The reader is referred to the work of Langsley & Hoult in this field. Generally speaking, however, the psychotic tend to be excluded by the psychotherapeutically inclined because they are considered to lack the insight and motivation necessary for intervention. I will shortly argue that this is not the case. The three groups I will discuss below are drug addicts, the psychotic and the elderly. I will describe the logistics of the service followed by an overview of its philosophy of practice and summarise the evidence for its effectiveness.

Heroin addiction

The drug unit at St. Clement's hospital in East London was run as a Crisis Centre, open 6 days a week, where addicts could drop in without appointment and see a doctor, nurse or for that matter have a bath, a meal, or play ping-pong. The line between treatment and socialisation was deliberately blurred as a means of entering the social field of the addict. They could register as an addict and receive daily supplies of heroin on condition that they attend a weekly therapeutic group, saw their doctor and key worker at arranged intervals, carried out prescribed pieces of homework and did not engage in either selling drugs or violent behaviour, at least at the Centre.

The philosophy of treatment was not one in which addiction to drugs was seen as the problem; rather, that the addiction was a symptom of a disturbed lifestyle. The aim was to change the life style by way of stabilising their addiction. Contrary to current government advertising, clients were openly told that it was themselves, not their heroin that was screwing them up, and as a condition of registering and getting their supplies free they must enter a therapeutic contract to change certain aspects of their lives. The amount prescribed was initially lower than that demanded but a deal was made that if they changed some aspect of their behaviour they could get more heroin. Examples of behavioural change included: spending more time with their family; stopping barbiturates; reducing violent behaviour; rotating injection sites; etc. They were given a full physical, advised on fixing and site rotation and given a key worker. The keyworker visited them at home and at various known junkie venues such as around Piccadilly Circus, so that there was information available on street behaviour and drug sales. Most of the patients had criminal records for violent crime, and horrendous family histories of physical and sexual abuse. The women were involved, to varying degrees, in prostitution.

The initial goal of treatment was not to make addicts drug free, but rather to allow them to become stable addicts, using heroin just as many of us use alcohol and nicotine. By making heroin available on prescription, the drug pushers were wrong-footed, being unable to compete with a free health service. It cut the need of addicts to commit crime in order to maintain their habit. It put these deprived individuals in contact with a structure, a centre and individuals prepared to give them time, attention and counselling. There was a tension created between the structure of the contract and the psychological pressure of the patients problems, and the crises this generated were used as a means of achieving change. This humanistic and, in my experience, very effective model has been largely superseded by the police model which focuses solely on drug availability which in my view creates the very problems it sets out to resolve. This however, is a political rather than clinical decision.

Is the St. Clement's model effective?

A cohort of 150 patients taken into this programme were followed up for four years, and yielded the following results:
Two thirds came off drugs and stayed off for at least 2 years. Less than 10% died, and these mainly from barbiturate poisoning. This was a third less than the national death rate among addicts (Ratna, 1978).

Psychoses - puerperal psychoses

From drug addicts I would like to move on to postnatal women as an example in managing the psychotic. Between 1% and 5% of women are diagnosed as puerperally psychotic in this country and anything up to 40% get a diagnosis of postnatal depression, baby blues, etc.

Such reactions are assumed to be caused by endocrine changes in people who have a vulnerability to psychosis and the recurrence of the condition is seen as proof that the women are flawed in some way.

The service we developed enabled mothers to be seen at home or in the maternity ward any time of day or night, 7 days a week, within 2 hours of callout. Patients were always seen in conjunction with their family and the aim was to support the family in coping with psychosocial transition by developing a support network.

The crisis model we have developed to deal with the problem conceptualises puerperal psychosis as a family issue, where sleep deprivation and a lack of support, combined with the high expectation of motherhood in our culture, push a woman into crisis. Psychiatrists treat distress in the postnatal phase as an endocrine disease, yet the connection between hormonal change and behavioural disturbance is tenuous, and replacement of the hormones has no therapeutic effect. The evidence for sleep deprivation around childbirth is well documented. The connection between sleep deprivation and disturbed behaviour is also well established, not only from studies in sleep laboratories but also from studies on torture victims. Truck drivers are not permitted by law to be in charge of a vehicle

61

after just a few hours of sleep deprivation. Yet women who have days of acute stress on top of months of chronic sleep deprivation are viewed as mentally ill for being distressed at the prospect of being in charge of a demanding newborn infant. In our experience, restoring sleep and creating a structure of time with and time without the baby is a key therapeutic strategy.

From time immemorial every culture in the world has set up support structures around a new mother. In our nuclear culture women who have been through the alienating experience of medical childbirth are expected to be up and smiling with only short term support.

Childbirth alters the politics of the family. It places a hitherto independent woman who was an equal partner in a situation of dependence on the husband, with heavy pressures to be a "good" mother. That change is often abrupt and takes her unawares at an emotional level. If her husband and social network fail to support her both physically and emotionally, and there are doubts within herself, a crisis can ensue.

The key measures to resolve the crisis are:
1. Restore sleep and delegate child care.
2. Set up a network with the family or others to structure the post-natal phase.
3. Family counselling.

Post-natal psychoses invariably present as crises with huge amounts of anxiety about the safety of the baby. We feel that telling a woman who is going through one of the most central psychosocial transitions of her life that she is mentally ill, poisons the family at the child's birth and sets up a vulnerability for future breakdowns.

By framing it as a family crisis, the crisis model encourages self-determination and strengthens the family resources for dealing with physical and emotional problems in the future.

It is not enough to deal with crises in isolation. One needs also to intervene at a social level. When we began this policy, the National Childbirth Trust - a national organisation for information and education on childbirth - dealt only with women in their childbirth preparation classes. Within a few years, almost all the classes were couples' classes, and support groups for post-natal mothers became widely established.

Does this approach work?

In the 15 years we have operated this policy, not a single woman treated by us has needed admission post-natally, and only one of them needed admission 3 years later. No one has come to any harm. In a comparable catchment area population treated on conventional lines by drugs and hospitalisation, two women committed suicide and two babies were killed during the same period.

Treating psychotics in crisis is for me one of the most exciting aspects of crisis intervention. One can take a medico-social model as John Hoult describes in this volume, or one can take a family therapy model, as described by Langsley in his book (1968). Our research shows that crisis intervention dramatically reduces first admission rates and reduces chronicity (Ratna, 1984).

The elderly

The elderly are the clients most consistently rejected from crisis programmes. This is in my view not a question of their clinical unsuitability but an expression of the prejudice of ageism endemic amongst psychiatric professionals.

The aged are the largest problem facing the health service and their needs are the biggest challenge confronting innovators of psychiatric policy.

The aged are indeed subject to crisis. An analysis of all referrals made to us showed clearly that crises had precipitated their referral (Ratna, 1986). What stands in our way is the medical model which leads to nihilistic diagnoses of dementia that engender helplessness, hopelessness and despair not only in the patient but also in the professionals working with them. If one substitutes an older humanistic model that sees the disability of age as a normal process in the human life cycle, one has greater hope. There are two periods of dependency in the human life cycle: at the beginning of life, in childhood and at the end, in old age. Cultures all over the world have recognised this, and established customs of caring to deal with it. The two ages are not dissimilar: dements, like children, are doubly incontinent, don't know what the date and time are, don't know who the Prime Minister is, and often can't tie their shoelaces or wipe their bottoms. We don't demand that children be put in hospital for these deficits. Rather, we provide for them extensive systems of care. In the case of the elderly, what we are doing in hospital (at great expense) under the labels of treatment and care is little more than institutionalised sedation, which is costly, useless and worst of all turning human beings who need caring into medicated cabbages.

The crisis model postulates that referrals occur because of the absence of, or a malfunction in the caring network. The solution therefore is to explore how caring networks can be created, sustained and enhanced or substituted for in crisis (Ratna, 1987).

There are three stages. The first is a shift from an individual model to a family or network model. The second is the co-ordination of systems around such a concept; and thirdly the transmission of such a model into mainstream culture.

Does this approach work?

We replicated Sainsbury's study and showed that our admission, chronicity and death rates were lower (Ratna, 1986). It is natural to ask, what about depression? We don't see depression as a disease. Rather, we feel that the aged are an oppressed group: that more than half of them live in poverty, they have the poorest housing, lack heating and food and are subject to high levels of rejection and prejudice. To deal with the unhappiness that is an understandable reaction to loss, disability, prejudice and social deprivation as madness in the individual is in our view dangerous. We can but point to the fact that despite the massive use of drugs and ECT with the elderly, they have the highest rate of suicide of any psychiatric group. We don't diagnose depression; we use a minimal amount of drugs; we have never used ECT. Yet not one elderly patient under our care has committed suicide in 16 years.

Conclusion

You have no doubt spotted a central theme in the evolution of our models. In each case we have gone from an individual to a family model, and from a family to a systems perspective. We have shifted from treatment to prevention and from medical cases to political issues.

The limits of crisis intervention are political, not clinical.

We live in exciting times, in a period of massive social change.

Psychiatry itself is in crisis.

The institutions that have been the temples of our power for two centuries are being torn down.

The mad whom we expelled from our cities are once more manifest in our main streets.

As in all crises, we are faced with both opportunity and danger.

The danger is a descent into the hereditary-degenerative model where we replace physical containment with chemical restraint.

The opportunity is to evolve liberal, humanistic, life-affirming models such as crisis intervention.

Thanks to the pioneering work of the authors presented in this and the following volumes, crisis intervention has finally come out of the cold and is an accepted part of community programmes all over the world.

All I can say in conclusion is "carpe tempum" - seize the time.

REFERENCES

LANGSLEY, D. (1968) *The Treatment of Families in Crisis* New York: Grune &
Stratton.

HOULT, J. (1986) Community Care of the Acutely Mentally Ill *British Journal of
Psychiatry* **149**:137-144.

RATNA L. (1974) *Psychosocial Management of Heroin Addiction* Paper read at
American Psychological Association Conference, Chicago August 1974.

RATNA L. (1978) *The Practice of Psychiatric Crisis Intervention* Napsbury: The
League of Friends.

RATNA, L. (1982) Crisis Intervention in Psychogeriatrics *British Journal of
Psychiatry* **141**:296-301

RATNA, L. (1984) Family Therapy with the Elderly Mentally Ill *British Journal of
Psychiatry* **145**:311-315

RATNA, L. (1986) Psychosocial Psychogeriatrics *Geriatric Medicine* **16**,3:7-8

Ratna, L. (1987) Retirement Crises *Geriatric Medicine.* **17**,2:11-15

Family Relationships and Outcome in Schizophrenia Focusing the Often Unperceived Role of the Patient

Dennis Scott

The paper I present here had its origins in research seminars I shared with Ronnie Laing, Aaron Esterson, David Cooper and Russell Lee in the early 1960's. In line with the early development of Family Therapy, our seminars centred on an intensive study of schizophrenia and the family. These sessions were very charismatic. They led to an in-depth understanding of the patient and the role of the family in his illness. Later I came to realise a limitation involved. It concerns the idealisation of the patient who was basically seen as an innocent victim of his parents and of society. This diminished his genuine agency - his status as a human being. The status of the parents was also diminished - they caused schizophrenia. They were seen as being schizophrenogenic.

But from Laing I gained a valuable introduction to the place of perspectives in human relationships. From this I developed my Family Interpersonal Perception Test (FIPT) which is the main instrument in the research I shall present to you in this paper. The FIPT is concerned with the way people see themselves, each other, and their awareness about how they are seen.

In 1968/69 I introduced family work to my team at Napsbury hospital. It was quickly taken up by innovators in the team. We were concerned about the *image of mental illness* prevailing in our society, and the way it led to suppression of awareness about the patient as a person - this suppression leading to chronicity and passivity in the patient. The patient was still seen as a victim but we also began to see how far he determined his own fate. Along with our growing awareness of the role of the family in outcome, this was a very liberating concept. It took shape in the Napsbury Crisis Intervention Service. We went out into the world to see our patients and their families to establish a human link with them.

After I retired I was away in Germany for 3 years. On my return I took up work with the families of schizophrenics along with Lenny Fagin at Claybury hospital

In recent years my orientation has changed. I have come to realise that before working with the patient or with problem areas in the family, it is essential to identify and respond to the qualities of the parents. By qualities I mean objectivity, tolerance, compassion, forgiveness - strengths which can take a person beyond emotional areas. As I will demonstrate below, both the parents and the patient can influence outcome, but it can be crucial whether or not the patient supports his parents and in some degree sees them as good parents. If the parents withdraw, and if their lives are lastingly and seriously affected, the outcome for the schizophrenic patient is very poor. The dependence of the patient on his parents can be obvious. The less obvious, but critical need for the parents to be supported by the patient is clearly shown up in the research I describe here.

The psycho-social therapies which have revolutionised the family treatment of schizophrenia in recent years all emphasise the importance of a firmly positive attitude to the family. The family is no longer seen as schizophrenogenic, but often as being the main resource in treatment. Yet the contribution of the patient to outcome has hardly been studied. His role seems to be suppressed.

The vast majority of research into social therapies for schizophrenia and other illnesses considers only the attitude of the relatives to the patient. In Expressed Emotion research for example, only the relative is rated; the patient's EE to his relatives is ignored. The FIPT has the advantage that it is a self-rating test which is scored by the parents *and* by the patient, and can bring to view aspects of their mutual relationships.

In the original sample, the FIPT was used to identify crisis-prone families where the patient, through repeated crises, had developed an untenable relation with his parents. I will define tenability later. This paper gives outcome in terms of *relapse* and *tenability*.

The sample was 40 first-ever admission schizophrenics admitted from parental homes to 7 hospitals in North London. At conjoint meeting with the parents and patient, the FIPT was administered during first admission. We made a prediction from the scoring as to what would be the situation regarding tenability and crises over the next 2 years.

At follow-up 2 years later the FIPT was again given. A detailed record of relapse, symptoms and social and work functioning was made at both meetings, and also at intervals during the follow-up period.

The FIPT

Figure 1 on the following page shows the score form. It consists of 44 terms which the scorer can use to describe the person he is scoring, e.g. the patient scoring how he sees his mother. He scores only the terms he thinks apply by putting a tick in the column opposite the term..

There are 16 positive or "S" terms - "S" for Strong - such as SELF CONFIDENT, MIXES WELL OUT, RESPONSIBLE; and 24 negative terms such as EMOTIONALLY INADEQUATE, SECRETIVE, OBSTINATE, INTERFERING. The most negative are commonly used to attribute illness - the "I" terms - whilst the less negative are the "N" terms - "N" for Nervousness not amounting to illness.

Everyone, normally Mother, Father and Patient in this project, sits down together, seated so that they cannot see each others' forms, and completes the questionnaire by themselves and without discussion during the actual scoring.

They score on separate forms:

> How they see themselves
> How they see each other
> How they think each of the others sees them

These are termed viewpoints - five in all, including the parents' scoring of each other.

FIGURE 1

NAME _____

DATE _____

YOUR VIEW OF _____

Below is a list of description terms. Tick off those you think apply.

N Demanding		S Strong willed	
NE Popular		C Controlling	
NE Respectful		S Affectionate	
N Anxious		I Detached	
N Sensitive		N Uneasy with strangers	
NE Devoted to family		N Submissive	
S Understanding		N Obstinate	
S Secure		I Sense of isolation	
I Left out		S Mixes well out	
N Confusing		S Careful with money	
I Confused		I Self doubting	
S Generous		I Misjudging	
N Dependent		N Helpless sometimes	
S Self confident		S Open to correction	
S Sociable at home		N Easily led	
S Responsible		S Tolerant	
N Emotional		S Easy to talk to	
N Quick tempered		N Jealous	
S Reasonable		N Fear of control by others	
I Emotionally inadequate		N Nervous	
S Considerate		I Secretive	
N Interfering		I Suspicious	
N Timid		I Fearful	
I Inadequate in the outside world		S Reliable	

By and large, families of schizophrenics use:
 I terms to attribute "Illness"
 S terms to attribute "Wellness"
 N terms to attribute "Nervousness" not amounting to illness.
(This classification is not given on the actual score form).

It takes about an hour for three to score it. But many subtle features of family relationships show up in the course of giving the test and it is worth spending much longer.

The ratios

These are important. In this paper the test results are analysed in terms of a balance of the amounts of positivity and negativity expressed in a viewpoint. The ratios are a measure of this and are defined as follows: the total number of "S" terms divided by the number of "I" terms attributed in a viewpoint, gives the S/I ratio, and similarly for the S/N. Thus the higher the ratio the more positive the view being expressed. It is very simple.

Results

In what follows I will first consider outcome in terms of Relapse in the year after discharge from the first admission. In this period 21 of the 40 relapsed, thus 19 did not.

First I will summarise how individual viewpoints relate to relapse in terms of their S/I and S/N ratios. In the following analyses, in families with two parents, their scores have been amalgamated by adding them and then calculating the ratios, and termed "PAR".

TABLE 1

Mean S/I & S/N ratios of 4 viewpoints and relapses

	Relapse		No relapse		P.relapse/ No relapse	
	S/I	S/N	S/I	S/N	S/I	S/N
PAR/PT	2.07	0.98	5.19	1.98	.018	.022
PT/PAR	6.1	2.25	8.45	5.22	.05	.012
PT-EXPECT	2.06	0.85	3.39	1.46	.005	.005
PAR-EXPECT	8.21	3.05	10.94	3.19	.33	.2

Mann-Whitney U, values of p 1 tail.

Table 1 gives the data for the Relapse and No Relapse groups. In the column on the left are the viewpoints whose codes are given below. On the right are the p values giving significances for comparisons between groups.

The Parents' View of the Patient (the notation is PAR/PT): The parents in the Relapse group see the patients more negatively, distinguishing the groups at about the p=.02 level.

This parallels the basic finding of EE studies. We will now go beyond the EE approach which only scores the relative, and consider how far the patient's scoring about his parents relates to Relapse.

The Patient's Scoring about his Parents (PT/PAR): The patients in the Relapse group see their parents more negatively, significant at about the same level as the parents' scoring about the patient.

Thus the terms which the patient scores about his parents are about equally effective in predicting Relapse as those which his parents score about him.

Looking now at the SECOND LEVEL: this, the meta level, is how the parents and the patients expect the other to see them, termed in the Table PARENT-EXPECT and PATIENT-EXPECT.

The Patient's Expectation gives the sharpest distinction between the groups of any viewpoint, significant at the p=.005 level with the patients in the No Relapse group expecting the better view.
But the *Parents' Expectation* has no relation to relapse. This intimation that the parents are out of touch in some way is important and I will be coming back to it.

Thus far I have used individual viewpoints to analyse the differences between the two groups. I will now look at the groups as a whole.

Figure 2 (overleaf) illustrates the scoring profiles of the Relapse and No Relapse groups. They are composed of the means of the S/I ratios of 6 viewpoints.

The *vertical* axis of this histogram is the S/I ratio scale, the higher the more positive.

At the top is the World of Parents: How they see themselves (PAR/SELF), and in the No Relapse group, how they expect to be seen (PAR-EXPECT).

At the bottom, is the World of Patients: How they see themselves (PT/SELF), are seen (PAR/PT), and expect to be seen (PT-EXPECT)

The line drawn between the two worlds is the *Well-Ill-Line.* It is placed just above the World of the Patients.

NO RELAPSE GROUP: The patients see their parents quite positively (PT/PAR), around the same level as the parent's World. The patients also see themselves positively compared to the other group (PT/SELF), and the parents fully support this (PAR/PT). The picture is one of mutual support between patient and parents.

FIGURE 2

No Relapse (N=19)

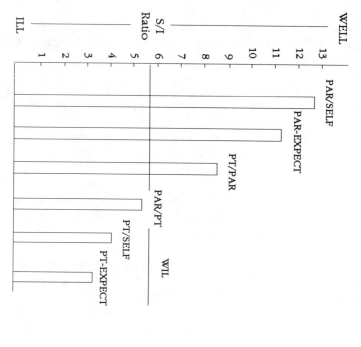

Relapse (N=21)

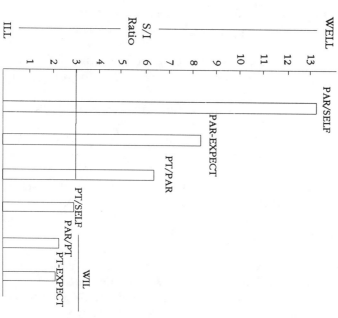

RELAPSE GROUP: The parents see the patient quite negatively (PAR/PT),
and the patients expect it (PT-EXPECT). The patients take a very
ambiguous view of their parents, seeing them midway between the two
worlds, that is between being Well and being Ill. Here there is mutual
negativity between patients and parents. The profiles will be clearer later
when I pick out the Untenable subgroup for examination.

Coming now to expectations: How accurate were the patients and parents
in their expectations as to how they were seen? I will examine this in some
detail as it has an important bearing on crisis.

TABLE 2

Correlation of PAR/PT and PT/PAR/PT

	No Relapse Group		Relapse Group	
	S/I	S/N	S/I	S/N
rho	-.26	.07	.58	.56
p	ns	ns	<.02	<.02

Spearman's rho, 2-tail p

Table 2 gives the correlation between the patient's expectation and
how they were seen by their parents. It shows that in the Relapse group
the Patient's Expectations are correlated significantly with how they were
seen, p<.02 for the S/I and S/N ratios. The patients are well in touch with
the negative view their parents take of them. However, for the No Relapse
group there is no correlation between these viewpoints.

Thus we have the interesting finding that the patients in the more
disturbed group are the most sensitively aware of their relationship with
their parents.

Concerning the parents

Table 3 (overleaf), shows that the parents in neither group are well
in touch with how they were seen; in the Relapse group they are
completely adrift in their expectations, which are even negatively correlated.

TABLE 3

Correlation of PT/PAR and PAR-EXPECT

	No Relapse group		Relapse Group	
	S/I	S/N	S/I	S/N
rho	.35	.25	.08	-.4
p	ns	ns	ns	<.1

Spearman's rho, 2-tail p

I will summarise findings to this point. In the No Relapse group, patients and parents are in general mutually supportive. In the Relapse group they are not, but only the patients are accurately aware of this. It is important to realise that a schizophrenic patient, despite symptoms, may have an awareness of his relation with his parents which they do not have of their relation with him. Without mutual awareness there can be no understanding between two people. I will look at this more closely.

In the Relapse group there are two subgroups in which the parents are out of touch in different ways: in one they over-expect the positive, in the other they over-expect the negative. Here, I will discuss the former subgroup, as it contains the 12 most crisis-prone families in the whole sample. In all of these the parents were seen negatively, even very negatively by the patient, but they expected a very positive view, 2-4 times too high. All these 12 patients after the first breakdown developed an Untenable relation with their parents. An Untenable relation is defined as one in which owing to recurrent crises in the family, the patient spent more than half of the 2 year follow-up away from home. Almost always this time away was spent in hospital, or in trouble in the community. The outlook for these patients is very poor. They are the patients who in past days became long-stay. This finding has been very thoroughly researched.

In order that the reader might get the feel of what is involved in the Untenable situation, he should try to imagine that he and a colleague get on badly and take a negative view of each other. You - the reader - are well aware of this, but your colleague thinks you take a very positive and idealistic view of him. If this is not possible to imagine, try it with a hypothetical boss or employer.

Here is an example from practice:

I have recently been working with a father and son. The father had early in life rejected his son and now wished to make it up, and he also wished to fulfill his own ambitions. He took his son home and fully supported him in taking a professional degree. The son broke down in an

74

acute psychosis. The father's belief in himself was shattered. He was on the point of seeking admission for himself. In the FIPT the son perceived his father's state very accurately, but the father, now distancing himself from the blow to his personal core, expected a pure positive view from his son, whom he saw in a totally negative way, as a mad and alienated person. The father was deeply threatened and the son knew it and was hostile to him. The father was unaware of the conflict. In therapy we contacted the father's qualities. He opened to his son in real forgiveness and understanding, but the son could not yet open to him, he had not forgiven his father. Unless communication and understanding between them can be reached the outlook for the son is very poor. This is a typical Untenable situation, excepting that the father could open more easily than usual. (For FIPT profile see "N.W., Jan '90", included as Appendix I).

In the research sample there are 13 families like this.

Figure 3 (overleaf) shows the situation for them.. On the right is the profile of the 13 with Untenable situations and Discordant scores, twelve in the Relapse group.

The profile on the left is that of the 27 families in the remainder of the sample.

The profiles show that the patients are seen more negatively in the Untenable group, and, as we have seen, they are very well aware of this. But the greatest difference is the tremendous gap between *How the Patient sees his Parents* and the *Parent's World.* The Patient has dragged his Parents down into the Patient's World. It is this gap, and the parents' unawareness of it, which makes the situation so liable to crisis. There is in fact a severe *disjunction* between the two worlds. On the FIPT this disjunction is indicated by a *discordant score* based on a number of factors of which the most reliable is a score where the patient sees his parents more than 20% worse than they expect.

The matter for these parents in the untenable situation can be critical. Parents are always threatened by a psychotic breakdown in one of their children, but in this group, one or occasionally both parents are deeply and existentially threatened. Their survival certainly as parents, and even as persons, seems to be at stake.

Furthermore, we have seen how the patient is likely to have an awareness of the parents which they do not have of him; this puts him in a position to use his psychosis to threaten his parents. In this way, in the Untenable group the patient's agency is put in the service of increasing his illness and disabling his family.

Therapy in the crisis situation

I will say a few words about the implications for therapy in the crisis situation arising from these findings. Here I wish to acknowledge a debt to Ian Falloon, some of whose Behaviouristic approaches Lenny Fagin and I have found useful.

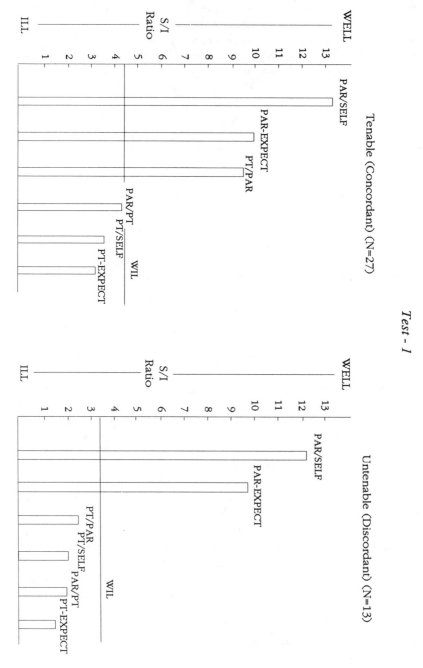

FIGURE 3

Test - 1

Tenable (Concordant) (N=27)

Untenable (Discordant) (N=13)

In the Untenable situation, with crisis never far away, we have seen how the parents will be deeply threatened and probably quite unrealistic about how they are placed with the patient; how there may be a severe disjunction between their two worlds.

In therapy it is a big mistake to try to close this gap by bringing reality to the situation through confrontation between them and the patient. This way leads to crisis and relapse.

In treating such a disjunction we must first support the parents by establishing a strong structure in which the therapist firmly places himself, along with the authority of the organisation he represents eg. the hospital. This strengthens the parental situation. It gives them the confidence that the world is not about to collapse. These parents often believe that every day may be the last: whether there is a future depends on how the patient is, and they may have closed the future on the defensive conviction that he will not recover. There is frequently an associated sense of doom surrounding these families.

The strengthening of the parental situation enables the patient to feel safe enough to begin to show himself. We may then begin to recognise his agency and motivation as he emerges from behind the psychosis. When a person is psychotic his delusions and hallucinations appear as autonomous processes. On emerging we may find him taking a part in his illness. At first we may find the patient threatening to "do it again". It is essential to try to get the parents to understand what is happening and not reject the patient, and we give the patient recognition for daring to come forward and show himself. The issue here may require delicate balance between recognition and control of negative behaviour. This path gives the patient a chance to actively emerge from the psychosis and take a step beyond the chronicity which often attends the Untenable situation.

Note: The patients in the project on which this study is based were admitted to 7 traditional hospitals in North London. There is evidence from other work I have undertaken that hospitals with a more flexible policy, especially over admission and discharge, lead to the patterns of family relationship described in this paper being less polarised, less black and white.

The patients and their families who took part in the project received normal hospital treatment, mainly tranquillisers and some social support. There was no special intervention by the research team, although we kept regular contact with those involved with the patients and their families.

The 13 patients with Untenable situations and Discordant scores in Figure 2, appeared at the 2-year follow-up to be deeply fixed in their Untenability. There were also 4 families with Untenable situations at the start who changed over to a Tenable situation and a Concordant score during the 2-year follow-up. Three of these had very good outcomes. Thus, there is a trend over time to move towards Tenability and Concordancy in about a quarter of families over 2 years.

APPENDIX I

NW JAN 1990

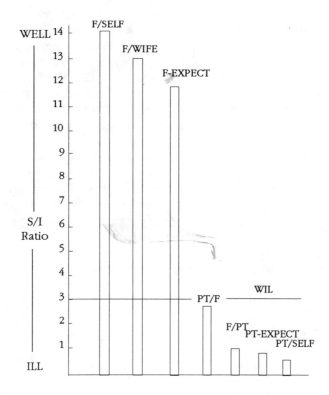

Crisis Intervention Techniques for Hallucinating Patients and their Relatives

Jack A. Jenner

The following paper will deal mainly with the problems of everyday practice in crisis intervention. Before discussing various interventions, however, I would like to start with a historical review of theoretical concepts of hallucinations.

Throughout history, people have been hearing voices and have had visions that are neither heard nor seen by their fellow-men. The importance given to hallucinatory experiences and the explanations that have been extended have changed tremendously over the centuries. Hallucinating persons are worshipped in some cultures and religious groups as the chosen, and cursed in others. Sarbin & Juhasz (1967) start their historical review of the concept of hallucination with the fathers of the church. Mystics, like St. Augustine, distinguished three levels of "vision". The mere perception of external objects was seen as the lowest level, the next was an internal representation or image, and last and most superior was intuitive understanding. The scholastics, like St. Thomas Aquinas, replaced the mystical concept of a perceptual continuity by a sharp bipartition. They distinguished between normal perception and perception of supernatural experiences. While the level of experience was the most important for the mystics, the scholastics gave more importance to source and content. The scholastical division of experiences into those of Godly and Devilish origin legalised the work of inquisitors. When, during the Renaissance, the power of the Church was taken over by citizens, religious concepts and explanations were exchanged for natural-scientific ones, which have opened the way for a medical concept. Today's palette of psychiatric theories consists of: biological ones (genetic, brainstem disregulation, disinhibition of cortical areas, hemispheric dysfunction, dysregulations of serotonin, dopaminergic or endorphin levels); psychological ones (classical and operant conditioning, seepage of pre-conscious mental activities into consciousness, abnormal mental imagery); and social ones.

In spite of our increased knowledge, the debate on (ab)normality of hallucinations and the distinction between Godly messages and mental illness continues. The concepts have changed, but the problems remain. Perceptual inaccuracy as such is not abnormal, as we know from "magicians" shows, from meditation and from our hypnagogic hallucinations in dreamy states. The extent and nature of perceptual inaccuracies and their personal and social consequences form a distinction between illusions or misjudgements of perceived external stimuli and normal hallucinations on the one hand and pathological hallucinations on the other.

Are hallucinations common or uncommon?

In their extensive study Sidgewick et al (1894) interviewed seventeen thousand "normal" people. Almost 9% of men and 12% of women acknowledged having hallucinatory experiences at least once. Visual hallucinations were most frequent, followed by auditory ones.

More recent surveys give very similar results: a surprisingly high percentage of healthy people report hallucinatory experiences (West, 1948; Posey & Losch, 1983; Bentall & Slade, 1985). Substance use/abuse and somatic diseases (especially sensory disturbances), as well as psychological influences, such as meditation, may cause hallucinatory experiences. Sensory deprivation may be their common factor.

However, these experiences are, as a rule, of short duration and little personal significance. Feelings of curtailment and restraint due to hallucinations (and their intrusiveness, probably) differentiate psychotic patients from mentally healthy people with hallucinatory experiences.

Crisis intervention and diagnosis

No therapy should be carried out and no intervention made without a proper diagnosis. However, the traditional psychiatric diagnoses, on which "regular therapies" are based, have only limited use for crisis intervention. Moreover, crisis situations most often do not permit a thorough and lengthy diagnosis; rather they require rapid interventions. Further, the disturbed reality-testing of psychotic patients is, more than in other crises, a complicating factor in the initial phase of establishing contact.

Here-and-now factors such as social support networks, patterns of interacting, reinforcement cycles, etc. give more useful information for crisis intervention. The importance of making various aspects of hallucinations concrete and monitoring them will become clear when we discuss the interventions.

Space does not allow further elaborations on diagnosis; suffice to say that most sophisticated psychiatric classifications are of little help to the crisis therapist, because they have only restrictive value in terms of what must be done. Life-threatening illnesses, suicide and homicide should of course be recognised, as well as intoxication, delirium, mania, and other clinical pictures that require direct actions.

Crisis intervention techniques

Crisis therapists have at their disposal drugs, psychiatric admission, psychological and social interventions. Of these only the (side) effects of drugs have been examined in double-blind trials. Opinions differ as to the (side) effects, the indications and contra-indications of the other three groups.

Drug therapies

Although hallucinations of patients diminish significantly on placebo treatment (Goldberg et al, 1965), neuroleptics have a significantly greater effect (Klein & Davis, 1969; Anderson et al, 1976). If hallucinations are judged to be symptoms of depression, anti-depressants may be prescribed either alone or in combination with neuroleptics.

Despite the apparent success of antipsychotic drugs in the treatment of hallucinations and in reducing psychotic relapse, some caution is in order. Drugs may cause serious side effects, particularly when used over longer periods of time. The results of the trial of Crow et al (1986) raise questions about the protective effect of neuroleptics against relapse. Negativism and non-compliance further reduce therapeutic effectiveness. Finally, we have to be aware that psychiatric treatment is mainly based on the assumption that hallucinations are symptoms of neurobiological processes that cause psychiatric diseases. This has directed our efforts towards a drug regime aimed at complete removal of psychotic features. However, our assumption may be wrong. It might well be that psychological processes cause biological changes that in turn "cause" hallucinations.

We may conclude that a substantial percentage of patients can neither be helped by drugs nor by psychiatric admission; that both drugs and psychiatric admission, in spite of their effectiveness, cause serious side effects. Hence we need other kinds of interventions too.

In our search for effective interventions we are confronted with three problems. Firstly, a comprehensive theory explaining the genesis of hallucinations, from which we could develop interventions, is absent. Secondly, the effect of some interventions is contradictory to theoretical predictions. Finally, most of the interventions that have been reported as effective were carried out with admitted patients. Most of them are single case reports and authors record contradictory results. Only a few studies mention the effectiveness of crisis intervention for out-patients.

Having delineated our limitations, we now turn to the available material. An important source are the reports of non-patients (Romme, Escher & Habets, 1988) as well as patients on the ways by which they cope with their hallucinations (Falloon & Talbot, 1981; Cohen & Berk, 1985; Tarrier, 1987). It is of interest to note the congruence between these coping strategies and those discussed in our second source: reports of psychological and social interventions. Below I will present an outline of both the coping strategies and the therapeutic interventions that have been reported as effective against hallucinations. Because of the limitations already mentioned I can neither give a systematic classification, nor indications or contra-indications. Further research is needed to study these.

Coping strategies

Recent literature shows that both psychotic persons and non-patients find ways to cope with their hallucinations (Falloon & Talbot, 1981; Cohen & Berk 1985; Tarrier, 1987; Romme, Escher & Habets, 1988). Falloon & Talbot (1981) interviewed 40 schizophrenic patients and distinguished three categories of coping: (a) behaviour changes: all patients showed some behaviour change contingent upon "voices", but many of them were unconscious of their contingent behaviours of which most had become habitual; (b) changes in physiological arousal: reduction (78%), mainly in sleeping and relaxation, and increase (65%), mainly in physical exercises; and (c) cognitive strategies: reduced attention (73%), acceptance (35%), reasoning (23%), and suppression (20%). Similar findings were described by Tarrier (1987), who interviewed schizophrenic patients with delusions and hallucinations. Patients who used several strategies seemed to be more successful. A relation has been found between preference of coping methods and profession, social status, sex, marital status; no relationship could be found between diagnosis and preference (Cohen & Berk, 1985). Schizophrenic patients use various coping methods, but less consistently than other patients (Cohen & Berk, 1985).

As little is known about the effectiveness of these coping mechanisms as about the way they work. Even the subdivisions used may be questioned: initiating contact may be listed as behaviour change as Falloon & Talbot (1981) do, but explanations in terms of change-in-physiological-arousal, and thought-distraction, a cognitive strategy, may be defended as well. We urgently require further research into coping strategies.

These coping mechanisms establish a relatively acceptable equilibrium. Although one may doubt the level of adjustment, there are several reasons to examine these coping mechanisms seriously: (a) despite decades of research our therapeutic results are far from impressive; (b) the correlation between EMG activity of the vocal cords on the one hand and the subjects' self-reports of the duration and perceived loudness of the hallucinations as well as the latency period between their reported onset and the increase in EMG activity on the other hand indicates that psychotic patients may give more reliable information than we have ever realised; and (c) in the light of the resemblance between reported coping behaviours and effective psychological interventions we may regret that psychotic behaviour was not examined earlier for its possible contribution to our understanding.

These coping mechanisms very much resemble the psychotherapeutic interventions that have been developed over the last two decades. It seems that our patients can teach us some lessons in problem solving. A combination of their experience and our knowledge may speed up the development of effective interventions. This may need a change in the ways in which we approach the "psychotic-reality". If we stick to our diagnostic definitions we cannot but accept the existence of two realities, ours and a psychotic one; the latter being unknown to us. It follows that the patient is requested to give concrete form to what he experiences. He is asked to describe what happens when and where, his reactions and those of others, and to monitor his hallucinations.

Psychological interventions

Several interventions, like monitoring, operant conditioning, systematic desensitisation, satiation, counter-stimulation and aversion have been described as effective by behaviour therapists. They approach hallucinations as forms of learned behaviour. Their theoretical explanations are general learning theories, and most of these explanations are given post hoc. That applies too for general systems theory and communications theory in explaining the effects of "prescribing the symptom", "mothering" and "horror" (see below).

Monitoring: Concurrent monitoring of hallucinations has been found to reduce the frequency of hallucinatory experiences (Reybee & Kinch, 1973; Moser, 1974; Jenner, 1984, 1988). Form and timing of the self-monitoring procedure are of crucial importance. Retrospective monitoring, diaries, and irregular monitoring either give no results or may even increase the symptom (Cohen & Berk, 1985). Some patients may object to monitoring out of fear of losing their "advisory voices". Subdividing voices into nasty and friendly ones may motivate the patient to monitor (Jenner, 1988). Self-monitoring may be seen as a cognitive intervention that requires a person to focus attention, and thus indirectly forces confrontation with reality. In my experience, patients show increased willingness to accept other interventions after having monitored their hallucinations as described above.

Operant Conditioning: Selective reinforcement of counter-stimulation (vocalisation of auditory hallucinations: Lindsley, 1963), or relabelling "voices" as thoughts (Nydegger, 1972) and punishment by contingent "time-out" have been reported as successful in clinical settings with chronic patients (Nydegger, 1972; Anderson & Alpert, 1974). If possible, relabelling as a form of verbal conditioning should be tried (Nydegger, 1972; Jenner, 1988). It is important that the environment is organised according to the programme. If not, the wrong behaviour may be reinforced, which may result in an increase of hallucinatory experiences. Although this is a tall order for out-patients, positive results have been reported (Jenner, 1982, 1984, 1988 & 1989).

Some patients report "withdrawal from contact"; this may be seen as a kind of "time out". They tend to do it irregularly and inconsistently.

Systematic Desensitisation: Successful systematic desensitisations to anxiety provoking and stressful situations have been described for hallucinations that are triggered by external or internal stressful stimuli (Slade & Bentall, 1988). The patients' coping equivalents such as relaxation and sleep are used fairly commonly (73%), but are reported to be rather ineffective (Falloon & Talbot, 1981). Possible explanation for this ineffectiveness are that the contingent behaviour has become habitual and is not consciously related to changes in hallucinatory experiences. The tolerant support of a therapist, and active coping rather than passivity and avoidance through sleep are further differences between systematic desensitisation and coping strategies.

Satiation: The effectiveness of exposure and satiation in the treatment of different anxiety disorders has been documented convincingly. Success depends on the level of arousal and the duration of exposure. The treatment of hallucinations by satiation was described by Glaister (1985).

"Prescribing the symptom" also has, besides its communicative aspects, an element of satiation. The patient is requested to hallucinate intentionally at agreed times and to intensify his hallucinations whenever they occur (Haley, 1963). Reduction and successful elimination of visual and auditory hallucinations were reported (Jenner & Henneberg, 1982; Jenner, 1988). In my experience the first trial of summoning hallucinations should be done in the direct presence of the therapist. His reactions may turn the tide for the patient as well as for the relatives. Attempting to evoke hallucinations will give rise to one of three outcomes: they occur, they don't, or the patient gets a message that the therapist is not trustworthy. When they occur the suggestion is given that this is a first sign of control; further summoning is done (=satiation). In the second case, which is the most common, the suggestion of control is given in combination with comments on the possible effectiveness of this strategy for taking over command of the "voices". The patient is requested to repeat the procedure. I have noticed that patients are more willing to accept drugs after this positive feeling of mastery. They are offered neuroleptics "to improve their recently acquired capacity" (positive relabelling). If, which happens relatively infrequently, voices tell the patient that the therapist cannot be trusted, the therapist suggests a relabelling of this as "a possible sign of fear amongst the voices, who have noticed that you have changed" (Jenner, 1988).

Aversion: Administering an unpleasant stimulus at the beginning of a hallucination until it subsides can effectively reduce hallucinations, but is no more effective than pseudo-aversive therapy (Weingaertner, 1971). It will be obvious that this strategy is hardly applicable for ambulatory patients and certainly not in crises.

"Horror" (Ferreira, 1959) may be seen as indirect covert aversion. It has been proven useful in cases of severe self-neglect. Contrary to its name the intervention is not meant as a deterrent; rather, it is based in caring. Two examples: we informed the mother of a patient who had torn his nails, yet refused treatment, our worries about infection. We projected complications that could be expected to occur in the future to the here and now. We conveyed the message that we wanted to protect her son against the agony of pain, inflammation and gangrene. Explicit deterring and moralising have to be avoided as they have proved to be counterproductive. An indirect way of communication is chosen in order to avoid a direct confrontation with the patient which may result in rejection. The patient described above accepted care and neuroleptic drugs as protective methods against infection. We were also able to mobilise a woman, who rejected help because her "voices" told her to stay in bed and forbade her to eat and drink, by explaining to her husband the agony of dehydration, thrombosis and open sores. She accepted drugs and agreed to evoke her voices as mentioned above (Jenner, 1988).

Ear Plug: According to Green's theory of defective interhemispheric transfer and integration in schizophrenia (1978) an earplug was placed successfully in the left ear of patients with auditory hallucinations (Morley, 1987). Contradictory to the theory, the effect also occurred when the plug was switched to the right ear. Blocking of ears and closing the eyes were reported in 15% of Falloon & Talbot's cases. In my own experience, quite a few patients refused to try to block their ears.

Counter-stimulation is another form of effective treatment for auditory hallucinations. Listening to a "Walkman" is a passive form; active forms are humming and singing. Only 13% of the patients of Falloon & Talbot (1981) practised loud stimulating music as a coping method. The proven effectiveness of both music (reward) and white noise (aversion) confuses the finding of a possible underlying therapeutic mechanism.

Thought Stopping: Wolpe (1973) instructed patients with obsessional ruminations to shout "STOP" whenever an obsessive thought came to mind. Positive results of this thought stopping have also been described in the treatment of hallucinating patients with obsessional thinking (Samaan, 1975; Johnson, Gilmore & Shenoy, 1983; Lamontagne, Audet & Elie, 1983).

Only a minority of patients attempted to suppress voices; their attempts were reported as ineffective. Reasoning, also done by a minority, was reported to give better results (Falloon & Talbot, 1981). Acceptance of the voices, including the acceptance of guidance, was reported by 35% and "appeared to minimise distress and slow the hallucinatory process" (Falloon & Talbot, 1981). Blocking of thoughts was reported by 73% of the patients they interviewed.

Social interventions

Training relatives in "selective non-reinforcement methods" is reported to reduce hallucinations (Nydeger, 1972; Patterson et al, 1976; Allyon & Kandel, 1976). These interventions have other effects too; in addition to changing the patterns of reinforcement, they also interfere with the usual patterns of communication, as with the level of arousal. For out-patients I prefer the combination of (a) prescribing the symptom; (b) detailed analysis of ineffective endeavours of associates; and (c) modelling them in selective non-attention to behaviour indicative of hallucinative experience (Jenner, 1988).

Different theories give different explanations for the effect of engaging in special interactions such as "time-out", and withdrawal from social contact. The problem is that none of the existing theories offer a sufficient and comprehensive explanation. Why do sheltered work, social activity programmes, and conversational skills training reduce hallucinations in some, but not all, patients? Is the central factor a reduction of "Expressed Emotion", a form of counter-stimulation, or mere distraction? Do changes in interpersonal contact restore the equilibrium between external and internal stimuli and thus prevent seepage of internal stimuli into consciousness, or is it simply that companionship fills emotional emptiness? We also know that subvocalisation precedes auditory hallucinations and that vocal activities (humming, singing and gargling) reduce them.

Mothering: Successful treatment of out-patients with Ferreira's mothering technique (1959) has been described elsewhere (Jenner & Henneberg, 1982; Jenner, 1982, 1988).

I am going to finish this section with three case reports that may begin to demonstrate how the various interventions discussed above may be integrated.

Case 1 - Mrs. Johnson, aged 50

A widow aged 50, Mrs. Johnson has a delusion that her extremities are broken. Self-neglect is alarming: she refuses to eat and drink, wets her bed and smears excrement on the wall. It is a life-threatening situation that can no longer be managed by her daughter and son-in-law. She also experiences three hallucinated "voices". She has been admitted to hospital six times under different diagnoses. Her last admission was almost ten years ago.

During the initial phase of the home-visit, she ignores our presence, although her reactions show her attentiveness. We, seemingly, accept the delusion and hallucinations and the way she defines their relationship to her symptoms. We bemoan her lot and pity her broken extremities, but stop talking directly to her (time-out) whenever she does not respond. We start to communicate indirectly. We tell the daughter (and through her, indirectly, the patient) the risks of dehydration, and paint vividly the agony of drying-up. We finish this so-called horror-intervention (Ferreira, 1959; Jenner, 1984) with an offer to do all we can to protect her.

Next, we request that she should move as little as possible (prescribing) in order to prevent further dislocation of "the fractures you feel, but we cannot see" (negotiating between realities). We then relabel her refusal to eat and drink as inefficient efforts to get her weight down (positive relabelling) and then lecture her on dieting. We offer something to drink and bring the glass to her mouth (mothering), while repeating our request to move as little as necessary to protect her fractures and as much as is necessary to prevent thrombosis and open sores (horror). She accepts. She also accepts "a good wash to prevent open sores" (mothering). She even agrees to take drugs "that may remedy her fractures". As you may expect, we prescribe a neuroleptic (reduction of arousal; Falloon & Talbot (1981) call drug taking a form of behaviour change).

The next day she has slept well and has accepted nurturance; she has eaten, drunk and has stopped bed-wetting. Discussing her "voices", she agrees upon evoking and monitoring (as described above). On the third day no voices occur. We praise her, but request her to try harder: "at least twice daily and when the voices come please keep them busy".

Within one week the crisis is over. At yearly follow-up for three years there is no relapse.

Case 2 - Joan, aged 16

Joan "sees" hallucinations of men entering her window; this began after her addicted brother's death. She holds the delusion that heroin-dealers want her to pay for her brother. She is followed by a limousine that nobody else can see. She does not attend school, and hardly sleeps. Her nightly yells cause quarrels with neighbours, who call in the police. Both parents and patient refuse the drugs prescribed by their family doctor.

All our interventions are rejected; she demands a full enquiry by the police, which her parents reject; whenever they want her to stop talking nonsense, she accuses them of neglecting her as much as they did her dead brother.

After an inventory of the problem-solving methods that have been tried, but have failed so far, the parents agree that confrontation does not help. The patient then acknowledges that we need evidence to convince the police. We suggest she should set a trap: several times a day she will call her intruders and photograph them (prescribing the symptom, satiation). Before doing so she will warn her parents (social intervention, change in arousal, and change in reinforcing behaviour), who are to promise her that they will safeguard her. All agree to monitoring. We see them each day in their home. The intruders don't appear, hence we suggest expanding the trap and propose that she should go to school with her camera. At three-year follow-up the hallucinations have not returned.

Case 3 - Patty, aged 30

Has been suffering depressive symptoms for the last three months. At night she has hallucinatory experiences: ringing of the doorbell, and hearing her father's voice, which she cannot understand. She awakes her boyfriend who cannot convince her that she may have been dreaming. Only after her friend has checked that nobody is at the door does she feel sufficiently comforted to go to sleep again. She has no explanation for these experiences, is not deluded, but is absolutely sure that she is not imagining things. We presume relational conflicts, which she denies.

We request that she should monitor her experiences and suggest she finds out personally who is ringing the doorbell, rather than asking her boyfriend to check. Her boyfriend may accompany her if she is afraid to go alone. The hallucinations disappear and have not returned after one-year follow-up. (Jenner & Feyen, in preparation).

Conclusion

None of the interventions described are typical for crisis situations, nor are they specifically designed for hallucinations. They have been found by trial and error. The only certainty is that they work.

We have not overcome the difficulties of establishing a therapeutic contact with psychotic patients (Jenner, 1988, 1989). Sufficient to say, carrying out crisis intervention with psychotic patients and their relatives means dealing with and negotiating between two different realities. Both "parties" need to feel that the therapist accepts them and their frame of reference. It has to be clear, however, that accepting is not identical to agreeing. Besides, accepting the perspective of one person might be felt as rejection by the other. We may lose a patient if we confront his defective reality-testing openly, but similarly may also lose him if he infers from our reactions that we are at one with others. He might even include us in his delusional system. We may lose the relatives by our attempts to establish a therapeutic relationship with the patient through insertion in his hallucinated reality.

We know that some coping mechanisms can be useful, but we are ignorant as to which, why, when and for whom. The effectiveness of drug therapy is proven, but we still can neither predict who will improve and who will not, nor who is going to comply with treatment and who will refuse. The effectiveness of several psychotherapeutic interventions has been described, but neither indications nor contra-indications are known. Research as to which interventions work for whom is needed. But what are we, therapists, to do in the meantime?

In the absence of a comprehensive theory we have to put together an individual treatment menu out of the many ingredients that may be effective. This brings us back to the beginning. Drugs and interventions are not the main problems of crisis-therapists; the real problems are: How should we establish sufficient therapeutic bonding? How can we motivate patient and relatives to comply with our therapeutic interventions for sufficient time to allow therapy to be effective?

In my experience skills in negotiating techniques, experience with psychotic patients and the drugs they need, skills in congruent and paradoxical interventions, out-reaching facilities, sufficient time, and continuity of care in terms of time as well as methodology account for better results.

Prescriptive intervention for hallucinating patients does not exist. Over the last two decades, however, intriguing and promising findings have been reported. Further research is needed to clarify the genesis of hallucinations and the mechanisms at work in successful interventions. In the meantime patients depend on our support and empathy, our endurance, our creativity, and our knowledge.

REFERENCES

ALLYON, T. & KANDEL, H. (1976) "I Hear Voices but There's no one There": A Functional Analysis of Auditory Hallucinations. In: H.J. Eysenck (ed.) *Case Studies in Behaviour Therapy* Henley-on-Thames: Routledge & Kegan Paul.

ANDERSON, L.T. & ALPERT, M. (1974) Operant Analysis of Hallucination Frequency in a Hospitalised Schizophrenic *Journal of Behaviour Therapy and Experimental Psychiatry* **5**:13-18.

ANDERSON, W.H.; KUEHNLE, J.C. & CATANZANO, D.M. (1976) Rapid Treatment of Acute Psychosis *American Journal of Psychiatry* **133**:1076-1078.

BENTALL, R.P. & SLADE, P.D. (1985) Reliability of a Measure of Disposition Towards Hallucination *Personality and Individual Differences* **6**:527-529.

BENTALL, R.P. & SLADE, P.D. (1985) Reality Testing and Auditory Hallucinations:
A Signal Detection Analysis *British Journal of Clinical Psychology* 24:159-169.

COHEN, C.I. & BERK, L.A. (1985) Personal Coping Styles of Schizophrenic
Outpatients *Hospital and Community Psychiatry* 36:407-410.

CROW, T.J.; MACMILLAN, J.F.; JOHNSON, A.L. & JOHNSTONE, E.C. (1986) The
Northwick Park Studies of First Episodes Schizophrenia - II: A Randomised
Controlled Trial of Prophylactic Neuroleptic Treatment *British Journal of
Psychiatry* 148:120-127.

FALLOON, I.R. & TALBOT, R.E. (1981) Persistent Auditory Hallucinations: Coping
Mechanisms and Implications for Management *Psychological Medicine* 11:329-
339.

FERREIRA, R.J. (1959) Psychotherapy with Severely Regressed Schizophrenics
Psychiatric Quarterly 33:663-682.

GLAISTER, B. (1985) A Case Study of Auditory Hallucination Treated by Satiation
Behaviour Research and Therapy 23:213-215.

GOLDBERG, S.C.; KLERMAN, G.L. & COLE, J.O. (1965) Changes in Schizophrenic
Psychopathology and Ward Behaviour as a Function of Phenothiazine
Treatment *British Journal of Psychiatry* 111:120-133.

GREEN, P. (1978) Defective Interhemispheric Transfer in Schizophrenia *Journal
of Abnormal Psychology* 87:472-480.

HALEY, J. (1963) *Strategies of Psychotherapy* New York: Grune & Stratton.

JENNER, J.A. (1982) Enkele Interventies bij Clienten met Mutisme (Some
Interventions for Mutistic Out-Patients) *Kwartaalschrift Directieve Therapie en
Hypnose* 2,3:212-233.

JENNER, J.A. (1984) *Opname Voorkomende Strategieen (Admission Preventive
Strategies)* Rotterdam: Erasmus University Press.

JENNER, J.A. (1988) *Directieve Interventies in de Acute en Social Psychiatrie
(Directive Crisis Interventions in Community Mental Health)* Assen &
Maastricht: Van Gorcum.

JENNER, J.A. (1989) Stationare Psychiatrische Unterbringung in den
Niederlanden und Methoden zu ihrer Vorbeugung *Verhaltenstherapie &
Psychosociale Praxis* 21,2:215-232.

JENNER, J.A. & FEYEN, L. (In preparation) Interventies bij Patienten met Auditieve
Hallucinaties (Interventions for Patients with Acoustic Hallucinations).

JENNER, J.A. & HENNEBERG, H. (1982) De Ambulante Behandeling van Acute
Psychosen (Crisis Intervention of Acute Psychoses in Out-Patients)
Kwartaalschrift Directieve Therapie en Hypnose 2,1:52-66.

JOHNSON, C.H.; GILMORE, J.D. & SHENOY, R.S. (1983) Thought-Stopping and Anger Induction in the Treatment of Hallucinations and Obsessional Ruminations *Psychotherapy: Theory, Research and Practice* **20**:445-448.

KLEIN, D.F. & DAVIS, J.M. (1969) *Diagnosis and Drug Treatment of Psychotic Disorder* Baltimore: Williams & Williams.

LAMONTAGNE, Y.; AUDET, N. & ELIE, R. (1983) Thought-Stopping for Delusions and Hallucinations: A Pilot Study *Behavioural Psychotherapy* **11**:177-184.

LINDSLEY, O.R. (1963) Direct Measurement and Functional Definition of Vocal Hallucinatory Symptoms *Journal of Nervous and Mental Disease* **136**:293-297.

MORLEY, S. (1987) Modification of Auditory Hallucinations: Experimental Studies of Headphones and Earplugs *Behavioural Psychotherapy* **15**:252-271.

MOSER, A.J. (1974) Covert Punishment of Hallucinatory Behaviour in a Psychotic Male *Journal of Behaviour Therapy and Experimental Psychiatry* **3**:225-227.

NYDEGGER, R.V. (1972) The Elimination of Hallucinatory and Delusional Behaviour by Verbal Conditioning and Assertive Training: A Case Study. *Journal of Behaviour Therapy and Experimental Psychiatry* **3**:225-227.

POSEY, T.B. & LOSCH, M.E. (1983) Auditory Hallucinations of Hearing Voices in 375 Normal Subjects *Imagination, Cognition and Personality* **2**:99-113.

REYBEE, J. & KINCH, B. (1988) Treatment of Auditory Hallucinations Using Focusing. In: P.D. Slade and R.P. Bentall (eds.) *Sensory Deception* London & Sydney: Croom Helm

ROMME, M.A.J.; ESCHER, A.D.M.A. & HABETS, V.P.M.J. (1988) *Omgaan met Stemmen (Dealing with Voices)* Limburg: Vakgroep Psychiatrie.

SAMAAN, M. (1975) Thought-Stopping and Flooding in a Case of Hallucinations, Obsessions and Homicidal-Suicidal Behavior *Journal of Behaviour Therapy and Experimental Psychiatry* **6**:65-67.

SARBIN, T.R. & JUHASZ, J.B. (1967) The Historical Background of the Concept of Hallucination *Journal of the History of the Behavioural Sciences* **5**:339-358.

SIDGEWICK, H.A. (1894) Report of the Census of Hallucinations *Proceedings of the Society for Psychical Research* **26**:259-394.

SLADE, P.D. & BENTALL, R.P. (1988) *Sensory Deception: A Scientific Analysis of Hallucination* London & Sydney: Croom Helm.

TARRIER, N. (1987) An Investigation of Residual Psychotic Symptoms in Discharged Schizophrenic Patients *British Journal of Clinical Psychology* **26**:141-143.

WEINGAERTNER, A.H. (1971) Self-Administered Aversive Stimulations with
Hallucinating Hospitalised Schizophrenics *Journal of Consulting and Clinical
Psychology* **36**:422-429.

WEST, D.J. (1948) A Mass Observation Questionnaire on Hallucinations
Journal of the Society for Psychical Research **34**:187-196.

WOLPE, J. (1973) *The Practice of Behaviour Therapy* New York: Pergamon
Press.

A Model for Crisis Intervention in Child and Adolescent Psychiatry

J. Stelzer

A description of the main characteristics of this successful model was recently published (Stelzer & Elliot, 1990). In this chapter, whilst referring to the model's "natural history", I will focus on the aspects of its functioning that made it successful; further, I will speculate on the administrative and epistemological conflicts that created the end of its operation in the setting in which it was developed.

In what sense was the model successful?

With a relatively small staff (1 child psychiatrist, 1 psychologist, 1 social worker, 1 occupational therapist, 1.5 teachers, 2 nurses and 1 child care worker per shift), we dealt during a period of three years (1986-1989) with a population of 200 inpatients and 500 outpatients per year. The age of patients ranged between 5 and 17 years, all of them suffering from severe psychopathology: 75% parasuicidal and suicidal, the rest being aggressive, psychotic, or severe non-compliant psychosomatic cases, or with severe learning disabilities. (A model for dealing with non-compliance according to the experience of the crisis unit and from an intersystemic point of view will be the subject of a future paper.) The model allows patients transferred from the emergency room to be managed with or without a brief admission period of 7-10 days, without referring them to other agencies yet providing a follow-up period of one year. The unit acted as the Emergency Service for Child and Adolescent Psychiatry for the entire population of the Province (one million inhabitants) without refusing a single case and with no waiting list. Only 8.7% of the referrals were readmitted. Also, and with no extra costs, the unit was used as a training centre for workers from different mental health disciplines and undergraduate medical students, as well as for research purposes.

My clinical and epistemological background previous to directing the unit

Directing the unit was an integration of previous diverse experiences. This can be summed up by saying that I was able to combine elements from both psychoanalytic and community psychiatric points of view. This was because of new epistemological insights that I had around this time. My first clinical experience in psychotherapy in Argentina was influenced by the ideas of H. Racker on counter-transference. Further personal developments convinced me that the regression of the therapist in the therapeutic encounter is as important as the regression of the patient (Stelzer, 1989). In Israel, using languages that were not my mother tongue, my work as a psychotherapist became more "global" and undertaken in a more regressive state of consciousness (Stelzer, 1983). There I was supervised by J. Issroff, a disciple of D. Winnicott, who helped me, through the use of the conceptual frame of the transitional phenomena, to be a very effective therapist and to manage severe psychosomatic cases in short periods of time (Stelzer, 1984). To work in psychotherapy in such a state of consciousness also allows one to perceive, through the loosening of interpersonal boundaries, the dynamic interchange of the inner worlds of the participants of human systems, and this was utlilised further in my work in the Crisis Unit during intake and discharge sessions by diagnosing and operating at systemic and intersystemic levels.

During my work with G.Caplan, I realised not only that different administrative settings produced different patterns of co-operation between child psychiatrists and paediatricians, but also that different administrative settings are necessary for dealing with different clinical conditions (Caplan et al, 1981).

Briefly, I concluded that to take into account in every case the interrelationship of the clinical, personal (of the treating staff) and institutional aspects would produce a more effective and brief therapeutic intervention. All this was translated into action in the model of the Crisis Unit when trying to construct an administrative framework that would be adequate to the task.

My previously mentioned epistemological insights came from a period in which I was working with psychosomatic cases, and I was frustrated by the difficulties of building a bridge between the epidemiological and empirical research and the actual clinical field. A personal talk with D. Bohm, then visiting Jerusalem, and the reading of an enlightening paper on new epistemologies in Behavioural Sciences (Delpech, 1984), opened to me a new horizon of operational research and other analogical, "right hemisphere" kind of models in mental health, as opposed to the "linear" empirical and epidemiological ones. In the future Crisis Unit the process of (1) explicating the working models; (2) its operational evaluation; and (3) further changes in the previous model, was a kind of continuous mental "emergency task".

First steps in the unit: Other positive aspects for building a successful crisis unit

1. *High Morale:* As we will speculate later, the high morale that we were able to develop was most likely the main therapeutic tool of the unit vis a vis very disturbed, hopeless, self-destructive teenagers. In the beginning, the morale of the unit was low as a result of staff members perceiving their roles to be of low status and the unit to be one which no one of my colleagues wanted to direct, considering such cases as the unit focused upon to be "social cases". In my experience, this low morale is a widespread phenomenon across almost every Crisis Unit that I have had contact with. It seems that the staff feel that they are dealing with the cases that "nobody wants"; ergo: something must be wrong with them as carers. Thus, in dealing with this low morale our tasks were (a) redefinition of the social meaning of our role: to convince myself and the rest of the staff that if we could find the proper

model, and we could do something positive even with the cases that "nobody wants", this would be very rewarding for both us as professionals and for the community; (b) to maintain involvement in training and research activities (we had a daily research meeting even in the middle of emergencies!); (c) to establish a leadership with the following characteristics: (i) a very democratic line of communication between staff members in which hierarchy was minimised; (ii) a clinical director who would always be available and be a presence in the front line, working with patients; and (iii) a leadership that would take on board responsibility, avoiding blaming the staff "under" him. We endeavoured to meet these goals, and our success in achieving them is reflected by staff turnover being nil and staff absence being very low during our operational period.

2. *Seniority:* The head nurse, some other nurses, the psychologist, the social worker and myself had already been in our respective professions for around twenty years. Crisis Intervention, as with any activity that requires the skill of fast and accurate decision-making, is not for junior professionals. First contacts with patients in crisis were made by the clinical director himself, with a senior nurse and/or the social worker, and not by a resident or student.

3. *Community orientation:* The clinical activities of the unit were not determined by any special interest of the staff members but rather by the needs of the population. Lacking incidence studies, we opened the doors to all patients sent to us by the community (and to those cases which our colleagues preferred not to deal with...). Determining what was a crisis was left in the hands of the community and our referring colleagues.

4. *Crisis redefinition:* The traditional clinical or psychodynamic methods of diagnosing and treating were not appropriate to our way of working. We did not asses or intervene with the child only, but rather with all the actors in the crisis situation, through redefining it.

5. *Continuous care:* We discovered that the best thing we could do for the patients and for the unit was to take care of clients ourselves, without referring them to any other department or institution. We provided continuous care, from emergency room admission through one year follow-up. Our experience showed that (a) the nature of the psychopathology (crisis prone) cannot be dealt with through the models of outpatient departments or residential treatment settings, for such patients are not compliant with a "waiting list" and "ordered" way of operating; and (b) if a patient has already been referred to those settings but has a further crisis, she/he is readdressed to the Crisis Unit and the process has to start again, but now with less control over the situation. For the above reasons, as well as for "selfish" ones (related to the need of the unit to control the situation) we developed a simple but efficient method of following up our patients for a one year period after discharge.

6. *Continuous explication of the model:* The ongoing questioning of the operational efficiency of the model in terms of its usefulness to the community and its epistemological coherence was carried out on a weekly basis in team meetings. The first written explication of the model was carried out after one year of functioning and was recently published (Stelzer & Elliot, 1990); for a more detailed description of the daily functioning of the unit, the reader is referred to this paper. The model was developed by extrapolating from some old principles of military psychiatry in dealing with combat reactions, some new developments in systems theory, through understanding the psychotherapeutic process as one of an informative experience that allows redefinition of the crisis in a more positive way, and gathering all of this together under the umbrella of a community approach that looks for a rapid reinsertion of patients into the community as its main ideological goal.

New clinical tools

In order to achieve the unit goals and to deal with our major constraints (community anxieties) we developed new clinical tools:

1. *The intake meeting:* Where in the presence of all the staff and all the actors in the crisis we tried to assess how each person defined the situation. We tried to avoid the Stanton and Schwartz effect (increase of pathology due to inexplicit and different opinions as to the meaningful people in the child's life).
2. *The discharge meeting* (attended by all those present at the intake meeting): Held after the assessment intervention period and in which the crisis was redefined, recommendations were performed and criticism of those recommendations, by their performers, was encouraged.
3. *A follow-up method included:* (a) An ongoing weekly family co-therapy session led by the clinical director and the social worker; (b) a weekly group for teenagers led by the occupational therapist; (c) a classroom for children not yet accepted by the school system; (d) 'phone follow-up of the family during a one year period, carried out by a nurse who reported any need for further interaction to the rest of the team in the monthly meetings.
4. No significant individual psychotherapy or psychopharmacological treatment was conducted.

Programme evaluation of the unit and its results

The programme was conducted mainly with a population of suicidal and parasuicidal patients; results show that after a brief period of admission the patients scored significantly less in the Hopelessness, Suicidality and SAD children scales, and results were positive on both patient and family satisfaction scales (Elliott et al, unpublished). Even though further research is needed, we could speculate, taking into account that few individual and/or pharmacological interventions were carried out, that participation in an environment with a high level of morale has positive effects and helped to increase hope in the patients.

The crisis of the crisis unit

After almost three years of functioning the crisis unit had to change its way of working due to increasing administrative and epistemological conflicts with the bureaucracy.

As we all know, conflicts between new and innovative clinical ventures and the needs of the administration of the institution in which such ventures are carried out are not at all unusual (Framo, 1976).

1. *Administrative conflict:* As we have said before (Caplan et al, 1981) every different clinical population requires different administrative structures. (a) As with all emergency work, the crisis unit requires a high degree of tactical-political autonomy in order to be able to make and carry through prompt decisions; (b) further, the unit needs a fast and effective networking system with other agencies beyond the walls of the institution that hosts the programme, and so requires many political contacts that frequently bypass the bureaucracy at, again, the tactical level. The bureaucracy does not always have a clear, explicit operational plan in which the strategical and tactical levels are differentiated, and this lack of planning and differentiation produces a situation in which the autonomy of the unit threatens the bureaucracy, and thus (a) and (b) become sources of important political-administrative conflicts. We are not criticizing here any particular person or institution; rather, we want to address our criticism scientifically towards some schools of management, as some experts in the field already have towards "Taylorism" and "Scientific Management" (Johnson, 1989). (c) The need to keep morale high requires that political information be shared with the team in a manner which conflicts with the general way of sharing information throughout the rest of the institution. (d) The emphasis on dealing with all referrals without increasing staff numbers attacks those sectors of the bureaucracy whose "raison d'être" rests in the political fights for getting increased funding for more staffing. (e) The Unit existed in a culture based not with its emphasis on principles of community mental health but rather on "client satisfaction", the "clients" being administrators of other agencies involved with the Unit. As this was at odds with our own philosophy, administrative interests often collided with our way of solving problems.

2. *Epistemological conflict:* Our way of working synthesised very old psychoanalytic and very new systems theory ideas under the umbrella of a community ideology and new operational and global espistemologies in a model that continuously questioned itself, and in which the classical way of diagnosing and treating were not central. This has not been the usual way of training our psychiatric nurses and

residents; as a consequence some trainees suffered a kind of cognitive dissonance whilst training with the unit, thus adding to the previously mentioned administrative problems.

Conclusion

Supposing that the above mentioned administrative and epistemological conflicts could be dealt with, our experience demonstrates that it *is* possible to operate an efficient community-oriented crisis unit for children and adolescents, offering continuous care from a small but senior staff, through (a) developing a high team morale; (b) instigating some new clinical tools for redefining the crisis situation; and (c) using a model based on new epistemologies.

REFERENCES

CAPLAN, G.; LeBOW, H.; GAVARIN, M. & STELZER, J. (1981) Patterns of Co-operation of Child Psychiatry with Other Departments in Hospitals *Journal of Primary Prevention* **2**:40-49.

DELPECH, L.J. (1984) Les Nouvelles Epistemologies *Annales Medico-Psychologiques* **142**:1063-1080.

ELLIOT, C.; STELZER, J.; CHEYNE, L.; & WILSON, K. *Evaluation on an Inpatient Child and Adolescent Suicide Program* (Unpublished).

FRAMO, J.L. (1976) Chronicle of a Struggle to Establish a Family Unit Within a Community Mental Health Center. In: P.J. Guerin Jr. (ed.) *Family Therapy Theory and Practice* New York: Gardner Press Inc.

JOHNSON, J. (1989) Introduction: Theoretical Developments in Psychosocial Work Environment Research *International Journal of Health Services* **19**:457-458.

STELZER, J. (1983) L'Absence de la Langue Maternelle dans le Processus Therapeutique *Genitif* **5**:80-87.

STELZER, J. (1984) Point the Vue Psychoanalytique sur le Traitment Individual et Familial de l'Anorexie Mental *Neuropsychiatrie de l'Enfance* **32**:291-298.

STELZER, J. (1989) Notes on Instrumental Dissociation and Psychosomatic Pathology *Free Association* **18**:2-72.

STELZER, J. & ELLIOTT, C. (1990) A Continuous-Care Model of Crisis Intervention for Children and Adolescents *Hospital and Community Psychiatry* **41**:562-564.

Crisis Intervention in the Emergency Room

Douglas A. Puryear

For the past nine and a half years in the Psychiatric Emergency Room of Parkland Memorial Hospital, Dallas, Texas, we have used crisis intervention as the central organising factor for our emergency approach. This provides 5 important benefits:

1. We can provide emergency psychiatric treatment rather than merely triage.
2. It avoids unnecessary psychiatric hospitalisation.
3. The approach is easily taught to beginning students, who quickly acquire an organised approach and increased confidence in their work, and develop skills which will be valuable for medical students going into non-psychiatric fields.
4. Having a central approach organises and provides cohesiveness for the whole emergency room staff.
5. Finally, crisis intervention provides an emergency room approach which is fun, rewarding, and often allows a real sense of satisfaction from having accomplished significant goals in a short time.

In our emergency department, each speciality has its own separate physical area. In psychiatry, we have 8-10,000 patient appointments per year. We are a major training site for psychiatric residents, third year medical students, and other trainees. Historically, in the United States at least, psychiatric emergency service has been limited to triage provided by the least experienced trainees consulting to other physicians (typical request for consultation: "come and get this loony out of my emergency room; I have sick people here"). With such limited training, time, and resources, many people have received unnecessary and probably detrimental psychiatric hospitalisation. By avoiding this, we keep psychiatric beds open for those who need them; decrease public costs; help the patient and family work out problems rather than postpone them; avoid separation from family, friends and job; avoid stigmatization; and support the coping skills of patients and their families when faced with problems rather than reinforcing helpless retreats into the hospital.

By demanding time to work with the patients, we can also carry out necessary evaluation in order to rule out underlying organic causes for their symptoms. The work-up is integrated into the crisis intervention; for example, as a way of establishing rapport, showing concern, providing a focused task for the team, patient, and family to work on, and demonstrating that the patient is seen as a valuable person. In addition, this approach yields a significant number of previously undiagnosed medical problems, preserving life and health, while providing valuable training and increasing the comfort of psychiatrically non-sophisticated trainees.

In our crisis intervention approach we try to work with the whole family. Sometimes family members have accompanied the patient to the emergency room and we interview them all together. We make phone calls to recruit family members into the intervention. We can use people to "create a family" where necessary. We use all available resources, including the family, friends and neighbours, the patient's therapist or counsellor, our nurses, churches, police, the hospital chaplain, AA volunteers, and on occasions other patients and their families or taxi drivers.

Our statistics show that this is a very effective approach to limiting hospitalisation. Since beginning this programme in 1981, we were able to diminish the rate of hospitalisation from 36% of patients to 10%, in spite of the fact that 12% of our hospitalisation patients annually are sent under court-order; we reduced their hospitalisation rate from nearly 90% to approximately 30%. In 1990, our rate has climbed due to deterioration in the community mental health services available for follow-up referral and to a legal change permitting involuntary hospitalisation for chemical dependency combined with dangerousness.

TABLE 1

Psychiatric emergency room 1980 - 1988

	PT Visits/Mth.	% Warrants to MDC	% Vol. Pts. Hosp.	Total % Hosp.
1980	643	83	24	36
1982	763	55	11	16
1984	884	49	7	12
1986	921	38	6	10
1988	810	36	5	9

MENTAL ILLNESS WARRANTS - 12%

We use a standard crisis intervention approach, and have developed a few stereotypic formulas, to be individualistically applied with flexibility and creativity for each case:

1. *Establish rapport and take charge:* In this stage we attempt to lift people's spirits, identify and emphasise their assets, and build up their self image.
2. *Establish a focused problem solving approach:* We frequently generate problem lists and pick some problems to work on.
3. *Make plans and assign tasks.*
4. *Develop a social network:* We assume that if enough people had been involved, or the right people, there would not have been a crisis; therefore, we involve more people.

100

5. *Provide support:* This frequently includes a referral, with our
making a telephone call after the appointment to see how it went;
6% of our visits are by appointments, with up to 3 visits for an
ongoing crisis intervention.

We generally use an indirect and a shot-gun approach. "Indirect"
implies using the power of actions over talking; for example, we do not
tell people that we are going to do problem solving, we simply begin to
do it; we do not say that it is wonderful that they are a carpenter and have
a close relationship with their cousin, we simply talk about their carpentry
and their cousin and convey that we are impressed. "Shot gun" refers to
doing everything at once, not knowing in advance what will work; thus;
because of the time limitations, we begin rapport building, history taking,
neurological examination, phone calls to relatives, giving of anti-psychotics,
calling in the AA volunteer, and setting up a clinic appointment essentially
all at the same time.

The psychiatric emergency room deals with all manner of cases, but
some of the most typical are: the chronic schizophrenic who is psychotic
off medications; the acute psychosis; the borderline; the substance abuser;
and the situational problem. These are not mutually exclusive diagnoses.
I will describe two stereotyped composite cases to illustrate the approach.

Case No. 1

A man is brought in by the sheriff. Quickly determining he is
psychotic, we begin neuroleptisation while attempting to do a neurological
examination, contact family members, obtain old hospital records, and see
if he has a current doctor. We attempt to develop rapport with him. As he
becomes better able to communicate, and the family appears or is
contacted, we find either that this is the first episode, or that he is a chronic
schizophrenic off medications. If the latter, we try to find out why he is
off medications now, and what obstacles there would be to his remaining
on medications in the future. We also try to find out the current stressors
in his life (questions of current stressors and why he is off medications now
are frequently related). We may have to deal with issues of his concern
about side effects, his doctor having left the clinic, his sister and her
children moving back into the family house, or his mother's pressuring him
to get a job. If this is a first break, of course there is more extensive history
taking and organic work up, as would be done on an inpatient admission,
with perhaps even greater focus on current stressors. In either case, the
family receives support and education and is involved in the treatment
planning. There is expansion of the network, appropriate referral, and
further planning of how to make sure the appointment is kept and works
well. For example, the mother of a chronic patient might be told that she
cannot expect to manage to get him to the clinic by herself, and is helped
to begin to recruit other family members, neighbours, church friends, etc.
to help see that the next clinic appointment is kept.

Case No. 2

A man is sent from surgery after suturing of his wrist. His wife has left him; he says he can't live without her. The issue of suicide is temporarily sidestepped while more information is gained about him, particularly focusing on his strengths and assets. He has children, so there are questions and discussion about them. He responds in a positive way, which initiates even further discussion. Later, passing mention is made of the irreparable damage done to children if a parent suicides. We eventually learn that his wife's leaving was partly due to her complaints about his drinking, although he vehemently denies being an alcoholic. We don't press that matter, but make a plan for him to begin attending AA, as a way to increase his chances of getting his wife back. Our formula is, if you want your wife back, what strategies would maximise the possibility of her return? This shifts the focus from the immediate - "I have to have her back right now or I can't go on living" - to a long range project. Then we ask if his efforts to get her back fail, how will he want to deal with that and what would he like to accomplish with the remainder of his life? He can always kill himself as one option, but there might be other options, or there may be some things to do before he kills himself, if that is his choice. Again, we emphasise the children (because he has a positive attitude towards them) and their need to have at least some continuing contact with their father, and how he can plan to see to that. (If he has nothing to live for, we might begin with the idea that he may as well spend time being of some help to other people, and develop plans for that). Our AA volunteer talks to him, and then our chaplain. We get him on the telephone to his sister, and get her and a friend to agree to go with him to his first AA meeting. We address other problem areas of physical health, employment, and estrangement from his family. We also see if we can help him to develop some short-term and intermediate-term goals for his life and consider what steps might be likely to lead in those directions. (If the patient had been initially unresponsive to our approaches, or remained sitting in a down-cast preoccupation, we would use the "chipping away" technique, speaking to him briefly from time to time while we went about other work, without trying to coerce him into talking with us, and over a period of time staging various interactions. The AA volunteer would visit him, then the hospital chaplain, then we would put him on the phone long-distance with his sister, then we might ask him to help another patient find a number in the 'phone book, etc. This non-intense waiting approach often works well with upset borderline patients.)

These two stereotypic composite cases illustrate much of our approach and many of our techniques, but the approach must be individualised for each patient. We find that this approach does not always work, and a number of patients have to be hospitalised, but with crisis intervention and a positive expectation, a number of patients who previously would have been quickly hospitalised can safely avoid that.

The staff obtains a real sense of satisfaction from seeing rapid and concrete accomplishments in the emergency room.

REFERENCES

LANGSLEY, D.G. and KAPLAN, M. (1968) *The Treatment of Families in Crisis* New York: Grune and Stratton.

PURYEAR, D.A. (1979) *Helping People in Crisis: A Practical Family Oriented Approach to Effective Crisis Intervention* San Francisco: Jossey Bass

PURYEAR, D.A. (1984) Crisis Intervention. In: M.F. Weiner and F. Guggenheim (eds.) *Manual of Psychiatric Consultation and Emergency Care* New York: Jason Aranson Inc.

PURYEAR, D.A. (1986) Crisis Intervention. In: G. Laux and F. Reimer (eds.) *Klinische Psychiatric* Stuttgart: Hippokrates Verlag Gmbh.

PURYEAR, D.A. (1990) Psychological Approach to Emergency Psychiatry. In: J.R. Hillard (ed.) *Manual of Clinical Emergency Psychiatry* Washington, D.C.: American Psychiatric Association Press.

"Crisis Intervention" and "Crisis Intervention Demonstrated", Audio tapes, Puryear Education Ltd., Dallas, Texas.

Crisis Intervention and Treatment of Parent Abuse in Japan

Yoshihiro Ishikawa

Parent abuse and the social situation in modern Japan

The number of adolescents either abusing their parents at home or refusing to go to school has increased so sharply in recent years that the phenomenon is now a major social problem in Japan (Bureau for Adolescent Problems in the Prime Minister's Office, 1982-86). For instance, over 42,000 elementary and junior high school students refused to go to school for a period of 50 days or more during the 1988 school year.

FIGURE 1

Change of number of school refusal

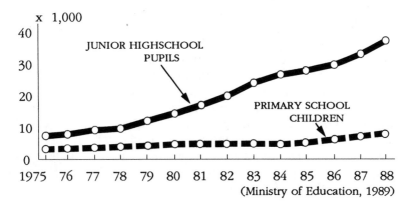

(Ministry of Education, 1989)

This is the largest number ever recorded since the Ministry of Education first started taking such surveys in 1966. Real figures are thought to be perhaps 3 or 4 times higher (Takagi, 1963, 1972), and it is estimated that approximately one third of this incredible number of adolescents abuse their parents (Aoyama et al, 1979; Uchiyama, 1983). Indeed, out of a total of 747 new patients seen by me at the Psychiatric Out-patient Clinic of the Tokyo Metropolitan General Hospital over the past 10 years, 118 of the adolescent patients (between the ages of 12 and 18) came because of refusal to go to school, and 37 of them (31.4%) also abused their parents. These 37 cases, along with a further 11 cases involving strictly parent abuse, make up the total of 48 cases in the "parent abuse group".

Why have these two phenomena become social problems? Children who had hitherto apparently grown up normally would actually seem to have problems hidden deep inside which are demonstrated by these two patterns of behaviour. In other words, we can understand these phenomena if we view them as indictments of the pathology of contemporary Japanese society which focuses so strongly upon the family.

We cannot discuss the continuing increase of parent abuse and school refusal without taking into consideration the tremendous structural changes that have taken place in Japanese society (Economic Planning Agency, 1983; Murase, 1980), namely, rapid industrialisation and technological progress. These two factors have caused too much importance to be placed on monetary and materialistic values, thus giving precedence to economic gain, as well as allowing the rationalisation of that precedence, leading to an elite educational cult, fierce competition in entrance examinations, and so on. All of this has strongly affected both the family and the individual, who cannot fight back. It erodes mutual trust in human relationships and is decisively a crucial problem in our society. Not only do these social changes form the background of parent abuse and school refusal, they are also deeply connected with such asocial behaviour as bullying and suicide, with anti-social behaviour such as shoplifting, bicycle theft and solvent abuse, as well as sexually perverted delinquency, theft, etc. (Family Court Research Association on Current Problems of Juvenile Delinquency, 1979; Wakabayashi et al, 1987).

Firstly, I will describe the characteristics and the circumstances of the violence involved in parent abuse which is so deeply connected with school refusal (Kahn & Nursten, 1962), and places such a heavy burden on the family. I will then take a brief look at its relationship to the personalities of these children, to adolescence itself, and to parental pathology. I will follow this with the presentation of a case study of a young man with a history of school refusal throughout his educational years, who violently abused his parents after dropping out of university. I will then examine statistically the prognosis of the parent abuse group treated by (a) the therapeutic team approach and (b) a psychiatrist only. Finally, I will discuss "crisis intervention" and treatment.

Circumstances and pathology of parent abuse

The number of consultations with children who are abnormally violent to their parents has been on the increase in Japan since the 1960's, although often these children are considered to be "good boys" in their lives outside the home. This new type of disorder, which went unnoticed before the 1960's, has been termed "violence in the home" or "parent abuse", to differentiate it from anti-social violence (Ebata & Takahashi, 1978).

Circumstances of parent abuse and characteristics of the children

In a typical case of parent abuse an adolescent boy suddenly becomes terribly violent over trifles, generally with his mother, and so cruelly and tenaciously violent that his family begin to doubt his sanity (Inamura, 1980; Ishikawa & Aoki, 1985). Characteristically, these children have, first of all, been overprotected by their mothers since infancy (Doi, 1973; Kawai, 1976), have had too much parental interference since entering school, and have warped parent-child relationships (amongst many others, Broadwit, 1932; Coolidge, Hahn and Pech, 1957), generally marked by the absence of a father figure. Secondly, whilst they are quiet, "good boys", they are also hypersensitive and timid, and display such personality disorders (Inamura, 1980; Wakabayashi & Honjo, 1987) as compulsivity with a strong wish for perfection, emotional immaturity and lack of perseverance. Thirdly, they are in the midst of the "autonomy versus dependency" conflict that characterises adolescence (Erikson, 1959; Masterson, 1972). When these three elements overlap, the child apparently becomes discouraged (Herbert, 1978) in the face of bad academic results, bullying by classmates and the like, and is forced to confront weakness in himself. He is then driven to bouts of anxiety by his sense of doom and despair. The feeling that he "can't take it any more" leads to a "dependent - aggressive reaction" which he turns against the object of his dependency, his mother, thus committing parent abuse (Takagi, 1963; Wakabayashi & Honjo, 1987). Parent abuse is a boundary which, when crossed, may turn the tables in the parent-child power relationship: either the parents fulfil their role as parents, or they are reduced to the status of slave to the child. While afraid of their child's violence, the parents also feel that they are responsible for this state of affairs, and, ashamed, they do their best to hide it and keep it within the family. This is why the phenomenon of parent abuse did not become evident earlier than the 1960's.

But in 1978, the father of an elite private high school student, unable to tolerate the violence that his son inflicted on his wife, killed him, and his wife later committed suicide. In 1979, a student at another famous high school killed his grandmother before committing suicide. In 1980, a student born into an elite family and long pressured into entering a prestigious university, beat his parents to death with a metal bat. With other similar cases following, the world's eyes suddenly turned to the phenomenon of parent abuse.

This reflects the severity of the parent-child conflict which can cause the relationship to deteriorate even to the point of murder. These cases of parent abuse within the home, which forms the touchstone of our country, rocked the very foundations of our society and many researchers started studying this important phenomenon from a variety of standpoints. For instance, Takagi (1963, 1972), pointed out that such parent abuse was proof of the disintegration of the structure and function of the family in our country.

Parent abuse and psychiatric diagnosis

Overt parent abuse is generally not the only pathology involved in what we call parent abuse cases. It is usually associated with a variety of other pathological factors that may range from delinquency to such mental disorders as neurosis, schizophrenia or epilepsy. "Parent abuse" itself is but one form of expression or symptom of some problem behaviour, from the psychiatric standpoint (Wakabayashi et al, 1982; Wakabayashi & Honjo, 1987).

I have seen 48 cases of parent abuse committed by adolescents in my clinic over the past 10 years.

TABLE 1
Number of clients by age-group at their initial psychiatric interview(%)

AGE		SCHOOL REFUSAL		PARENT ABUSE	
Early Teens	(12-13)	11	(15.7)	6	(12.5)
Mid Teens	(14-16)	43	(61.4)	28	(58.3)
Late Teens	(17-18)	16	(22.9)	14	(29.2)
TOTAL		70	(100.0)	48	(100.0)

Boys far outnumbered girls by a ratio of 7:1.

TABLE 2
Number of clients by sex (%)

SEX	SCHOOL REFUSAL		PARENT ABUSE	
Male	39	(55.7)	41	(85.4)
Female	31	(44.3)	7	(14.6)
TOTAL	70	(100.0)	48	(100.0)

The psychiatric diagnoses indicated neurosis in 34 of the cases (70%), and in the remaining 14 cases (30%), a noticeably large number, psychosis was diagnosed.

TABLE 3
Number of clients by psychiatric diagnosis (%)

DIAGNOSIS	SCHOOL REFUSAL		PARENT ABUSE	
Neurotic Circle	45	(64.3)	34	(70.8)
Psychotic Circle	23	(32.9)	14	(29.2)
Others	2	(2.8)	0	(0)
TOTAL	70	(100.0)	48	(100.0)

5 of these psychotic cases had schizophrenic tendencies and 5 were confirmed cases of schizophrenia. 1 suffered from depression, 2 suffered from epilepsy and 1 had epileptic tendencies. Consequently, any case showing abnormally brutal violence should be psychiatrically evaluated.

TABLE 4
Detailed diganosis of psychotic circle

DIAGNOSIS	SCHOOL REFUSAL		PARENT ABUSE	
Schizophrenia	13	(5)	10	(5)
Depression	8	(6)	1	(1)
Epilepsy	2	(1)	3	(2)
TOTAL	23	(12)	14	(8)

As I mentioned, 70% of the cases of parent abuse were diagnosed as being at the neurotic level. In these cases, in addition to the patient's character (Masterson, 1972), a number of psychological and social factors are thought to have entered into play, such as the parent-child relationship during the crisis of adolescence in 40 of the cases (83.3%) and problems at school in 26 of the cases (54.2%).

TABLE 5
Number of clients by family problems (%)

PROBLEMS	SCHOOL REFUSAL		PARENT ABUSE	
Apparent	45	(64.3)	40	(83.3)
Not Apparent	9	(12.9)	1	(2.1)
Unclear	16	(22.8)	7	(14.6)
TOTAL	70	(100.0)	48	(100.0)

TABLE 6
Detailed classification of family problems (%)

PROBLEMS	SCHOOL REFUSAL		PARENT ABUSE	
Dominant Mother	23	(34.3)	18	(31.7)
Dominant Father	13	(19.4)	8	(14.0)
Divorce or Conflict	4	(6.0)	8	(14.0)
Father Deceased	1	(1.5)	2	(3.5)
Father not Available	8	(11.9)	8	(14.0)
Dominant Grandparents	6	(9.0)	3	(5.3)
Conflict among Siblings	12	(17.9)	10	(17.5)
TOTAL	67	(100.0)	57	(100.0)

TABLE 7
Number of clients by school problems (%)

PROBLEMS	SCHOOL REFUSAL		PARENT ABUSE	
Apparent	48	(67.6)	27	(55.1)
Not Apparent	7	(9.9)	5	(10.2)
Unclear	16	(22.5)	17	(34.7)
TOTAL	71	(100.0)	49	(100.0)

TABLE 8
Detailed classification of school problems (%)

PROBLEMS	SCHOOL REFUSAL		PARENT ABUSE	
Human Relationships	22	(27.8)	11	(20.8)
Victimisation	10	(12.7)	5	(9.4)
Problems with Teachers	8	(10.1)	7	(13.2)
Poor Achievement	16	(20.3)	7	(13.2)
No Apparent Problem	6	(7.6)	4	(7.5)
Unclear	17	(21.5)	19	(35.9)
TOTAL	79	(100.0)	53	(100.0)

Crisis intervention and therapy in cases of parent abuse

Understanding the circumstances and the pathology of parent abuse does not, for all that, make the treatment easy (Ebata & Takahashi, 1978). Parents who go to a university hospital or a counselling centre are all too often sent away after being told "there is nothing we can do unless you bring in the violent child" (Ishikawa & Aoki, 1986). The medical model that has the patient himself as the object of treatment cannot be applied here. In reality, neither psychology nor education have as yet provided us with an effective therapy. Under these circumstances, violent parent abuse brings the household to the brink of destruction.

At such a time of crisis, how should we intervene therapeutically? What should the treatment be? How do we handle the family? I will try to answer these questions by presenting a typical case.

Profile and diagnosis of the case

The case, a male student enrolled at a so-called "cram" school, was 23 at the time of the initial consultation. The chief complaints were a refusal to go to school beginning in kindergarten and continuing through university, and parent abuse that began one year after dropping out of university.

110

Shocked and frightened, his parents had gone to one famous psychiatric hospital or educational counselling centre after another, only to be either turned away with the standard "you will have to bring the patient in", or made to feel responsible, being told "you did not raise him properly". No one gave them any concrete advice; they were very distressed and at a loss as to what to do. Quite by chance, a female case worker I had known for a long time introduced the case to me at a clinical conference. The parents, grasping at straws, somehow persuaded their reluctant child to attend and brought him to the psychiatric out-patient clinic.

Of medium height and build, the patient appeared to be an intelligent, quiet youth who answered my questions promptly and systematically. It seemed unbelievable that this youth was so violent at home that he frightened his parents.

The psychiatric evaluation excluded schizophrenia and manic depressive illness. Psychodynamically, the patient showed such personality traits as introversion, hypersensitivity, perfectionism and a strong tendency towards anthropophobia. His discouragement regarding his schoolwork and performance in physical education had triggered his refusal to attend school. When these combined with the crisis of adolescence, he became more anxious, more worried and desperate and I theorised that he was impulsively hurling his feeling of not being able to go on at his parents and the things closest to him. The diagnosis at the initial consultation was character neurosis. However, the possibility of borderline personality disorder could not be excluded as he was severely depressed, showed weak self-control, would become extremely angry or agitated, had attempted suicide, etc.

Treatment was begun after careful consideration of the various elements involved in the case: the patient's promise to come to the hospital, the parents' eagerness, the referral etc. As his psychiatrist, I teamed up with Mr. Shiro Aoki, a skilled psychiatric social workers (PSW), to form a therapeutic team, and undertook the therapy.

Crisis intervention

After 2 sessions, worried because his studies were not progressing as he wanted and dissatisfied with his parents, the patient abused his parents terribly at home and then tried to strangle himself. Both his parents were in a state of total confusion when they asked our therapeutic team for help. We judged this to be an emergency and the PSW rushed to the patient's home, a course of action which greatly eased his parents anxiety and for which they were thankful.

The patient had collapsed on the roof, a rope lying nearby. The PSW joined forces with his parents in carrying him quietly back to his room and putting him to bed. He then took the patient's temperature, pulse and blood pressure to make sure that there were no abnormalities. He cooled the patient's face with a wet towel etc., and gave him some antipsychotic medication on my advice. The PSW then went into the next room, which

111

was separated from the bedroom only by sliding doors, to be given an account of the details of the day by the young man's parents.

The PSW first explained the legal procedure compelling the patient to undergo psychiatric treatment whenever he became extremely violent or there was a strong risk that he would commit suicide. He spoke loudly enough for the patient in the next room to overhear him. He then told the parents: "There is something that this kind of patient cannot tell anyone, some pain inside him that even his parents cannot understand. If we are to understand that suffering and its cause, it is important that the parents co-operate with and help the professionals. It is important not to blame the child, who is suffering, nor to lecture him, or to consistently issue him warnings. At the same time neither should the parents blame themselves for the past or complain about it. If the child breaks a window pane, first ask him if he has hurt himself and try to understand why he had to break that pane. The parents should clean up the broken glass themselves and the child will then begin to help them. The parents should listen to their child attentively, do their best to understand his feelings and give him whatever support he may need. If parents and child act together, little by little, the rigid parent-child relationship will turn into a trusting one. Until then, it is important for the parents not to become anxious, but to listen carefully to whatever their child tells them. Such behaviour on the part of the parents often works better than any medicine prescribed by a doctor. I believe that parents are the best doctors".

After listening to the PSW's explanation, the patient's parents said: "This is the first time anyone has ever given us concrete advice", and deeply appreciative, they promised to their best and to co-operate. That home visit lasted 4 hours, from 12 midnight to 4.00am.

Following this incident, the patient locked himself in his room, stayed in bed and refused to come to the hospital. The treatment could thus only go on "indirectly", through the parents. As the number of interviews with the parents grew, I came to understand that the father had a tendency to progress from anxiety to mental confusion whenever the son exhibited abusive behaviour, and he was thus at risk of relating impulsively against the son in a life-threatening manner. The most pressing need then became the treatment of the father and his mental stability.

Our therapeutic team then suggested the following 3 points to support the parents in case of a crisis at home. First, they could call us in an emergency at any time of the day or night. Second, we would make "house calls" whenever necessary. Third, we focused on obtaining emotional stability in the father with the prescription of anti-anxiolytics and hypnotics. By both pledging ourselves to and acting on these 3 points, we obtained a clear improvement in the stability of the father, who had previously been severely anxious.

Having recovered his emotional stability, the father wanted to talk frankly with his wife with the therapist present. For the first time since their marriage, mother and father flung at each other the true feelings they had suppressed for 30 years. The confrontation was quite serious. It became clear in the course of this confrontation that a deeply-rooted conflict, which might lead to a divorce, had been developing between the parents. Through repeated, earnest discussion, and thanks to the therapist's efforts at reconciliation as well as the parents' trust in him, this crisis helped the parents to deepen their mutual understanding. Not only that, it also gave them points of reference from which to better understand their child, and the way they approached their son began to change for the better.

Treatment of the child and joint family therapy

The changes in the parents soon began to be reflected in the child who became more secure and relaxed. He began to criticise his parents in front of the therapist. For instance, he said "My parents have placed expectations on me since I was a baby, so I became what they wanted me to be. I did not like it, but since my mother kept telling me to "be grateful to my parents" I killed whatever feelings I had and didn't say what I thought". And: "My father used to lecture me patronisingly, saying that it was for my own good, to the point where I thought why should I go to school for that kind of father? When that feeling erupted, I refused to go to school and became violent towards my parents". These words were highly significant in understanding the mechanism of the onset of abusive behaviour in this child.

The PSW repeatedly listened to the child's excuses, accepting and supporting him. He then endeavoured to help the child to remember his parents good sides and their love for him.

Once these preparatory steps were over with, joint family therapy could begin. The child, supported by the therapist, fearfully started to express his dissatisfaction and anger with his parents. The parents then became emotional, criticising and verbally attacking the child. The PSW explained to them: "In family therapy, each participant listens and accepts what the other has to say and expresses his or her feelings openly. The important thing is that it should be a place and time for the child, who is in a weaker position, to get used to talking to his parents who are in a stronger position. The stronger person learns to accept the feelings and opinions of the weaker one. Even parents and children should respect one another's personalities."

This explanation gave strength to both parents and child who slowly became able to talk more openly, and on more equal terms. The parents came to understand the psychology of their child more fully, to see the suffering child that could not bring himself to go to school, and although still anxious and suffering, they were able to watch over him more calmly.

Over time, the parents and child overcame may crises, had many ups and downs, but gradually, the family found harmony, the child actively began to take part in social activities and the parent abuse subsided.

The relationship between a patient's treatment and what he has observed to be the cause of his problem particularly in relation to the family

The patient gave us his views on the relationship between the treatment he received and what he believes caused the problems of family violence he and his family experienced.

"I used to be terrible at getting along with other people, but it got easier for me (due to the treatment). I believe it was very important that I learned how to speak frankly with my father. After establishing this open relationship with my father I was able to concentrate on my studies as well as change my habits and the people I hung around with. Before, I would set extremely high goals for myself with the intention of accomplishing them, only to stop halfway through, thus getting myself into a panic and starting the vicious circle all over again. But now, no matter what happens, I have the confidence that things will turn out all right. It's not only because I have faith in my abilities, but because I know that whenever I need to I can go to my professor, my friends, my parents or my therapist for help."

The patient was able to give an objective evaluation of his parents' good and bad points.

"In my childhood, when I rebelled against the way my parents raised me or the way they showed affection for me, I ended up, in effect, hurting myself. I became emotionally unstable and lost confidence in myself. However, after exhaustively discussing the problem with my therapist and parents, I came to understand my parents' position as well as their love for me. Despite my refusal to attend school, and the violence I inflicted upon my parents for the longest time, they refused to give up on me. They suggested that I go somewhere for treatment, but always left the final choice to me, something I've always been very thankful for." That treatment was vital in giving the patient insight into the problem.

As a result of the treatment, the patient came to understand the feelings of anxiety he had always suppressed in regards to the distorted relationship he had with his parents. As the patient and his parents become closer as a family, the symptoms of violence towards his parents and absenteeism from school started to disappear. In addition, as the relationship with his father improved, so did his relationship with people in general. At the same time, he became more positive in his attitude and gained the confidence to try many different things. This is proof of the tremendous recovery the patient made. Mr. Aoki and I share the view that not only is it important to treat the patient individually, it should also be the duty of the therapist to motivate the entire family to co-operate in the treatment.

A statistical study on the effectiveness of the Ishikawa-Aoki team treatment approach to parent abuse

Our study consists of 48 adolescent clients. 21 were treated by team treatment approach. 11 were treated by myself alone. The remaining 16 clients had an insufficient treatment period, which made prognosis unobtainable.

The statistical breakdown is as follows. 9 (42.9%) of the 21 patients who were treated by our team treatment approach for more than 3 months displayed good results, recovering psychologically and socially. By this I mean the patients could choose, with some guidance, what course of

114

action they should pursue, continuing in school, finding work etc. 10 (47.6%) of the patients stabilised enough to regain control to the point where they could suppress their violent behaviour. Only 2 (9.5%) subjects showed bad prognosis.

TABLE 9
Prognosis of adolescent clients as of 4.1.90 (%)

PROGNOSIS	SCHOOL REFUSAL		PARENT ABUSE	
Good	28	(40.0)	14	(29.2)
Stable	8	(11.4)	9	(18.8)
Bad	0	(0)	2	(4.2)
Hospitalised	5	(7.1)	4	(8.2)
Unclear	29	(41.5)	19	(39.6)
TOTAL	70	(100.0)	48	(100.0)

TABLE 10
Prognosis of clients treated by Ishikawa-Aoki team treatment approach (%)

PROGNOSIS	SCHOOL REFUSAL		PARENT ABUSE	
Good	6	(50.0)	9	(42.9)
Stable	5	(46.9)	10	(47.6)
Bad	1	(3.1)	2	(9.5)
TOTAL	12	(100.0)	21	(100.0)

One of them was diagnosed as suffering from severe schizophrenia and has since required hospitalisation. The other was in a state of borderline personality disorder characterised by a sado-masochistic relationship with his mother.

In comparison with our team treatment approach, treatment by a psychiatrist alone resulted in 5 (45.5%) subjects showing good prognoses, but 4 (36.3%) showing bad prognoses.

TABLE 11
Prognosis of clients treated by a psychiatrist alone (%)

PROGNOSIS	SCHOOL REFUSAL		PARENT ABUSE	
Good	22	(68.8)	5	(45.5)
Stable	6	(18.7)	2	(18.2)
Bad	4	(12.5)	4	(36.3)
TOTAL	32	(100.0)	11	(100.0)

These results were therefore not nearly so successful as those achieved with team treatment. Furthermore, when I judged a patient to be too difficult to treat by myself, that patient was given over to our team treatment approach. Therefore, the subjects who suffered from more severe disturbances were treated by team therapy. In spite of these severe disturbances, our team treatment has resulted in better prognoses. It has been demonstrated that our team treatment approach to parent abuse was very effective.

The case history above and the statistical study have clearly shown the marked effectiveness of the team treatment approach. This approach made previously untreatable clients treatable, when other therapeutic procedures had proved ineffective.

Considerations on the Ishikawa-Aoki team therapy and its effectiveness

According to the patient's own experience and statistical evidence, we have found that our treatment method is very effective. Why might this be so?

First, we believe the make-up of the treatment team is fundamentally important. The team is composed of a psychiatric social worker and a psychiatrist, both of whom truly have the same perspective on treatment, as well as sharing similar treatment methods. Both members are independent and equal in status, but share in the information each has gained from the client's parents. They learn from each other, entrust roles and responsibilities to each other, offset each other's weak points and grow together. We believe the trust and respect team members show for each other are the driving force behind the treatment method's effectiveness.

Secondly, I hope that what I have said up to now will serve as a reference model (Kahn & Nursten, 1962), with regard to what it takes to re-unify a family, to improve a family situation. First, we build up a relationship with the parents. Having achieved this we wait for the right moment to establish contact with the child. In this process, all members of the patient's family, in the same manner as the treatment team, try to understand each other, respect each other, and help each other with important matters, as well as helping each other to become more independent. In other words, we act as a catalyst to release the hidden natural healing powers the family possesses.

Thirdly, in order to initiate the release of the family's own hidden healing powers, we need to deal with the atmosphere of emergency associated with the early stages of the treatment. Because the patient is an out-patient, the parents often have a terrible time with the child at home and are extremely anxious about the situation. So, in case of an emergency we allow them to call us anytime; we promise to come rushing to their house immediately if need be; and we offer advice, provide shelter and dispense medication if necessary. These specific promises are made and adhered to. Such promises and actions tend to calm the parents, strengthen the bond of trust between the parents and treatment team, and encourage the parents to continue the out-patient treatment.

Fourthly, we leave it completely up to the parents to decide which member of the team they would like to interact with. The reason behind giving this choice is that the main purpose of our treatment is to get the parents to act more independently, and ultimately, of course, to get the child to do so too. Once the parents are given the right to choose, they repeat the experience of taking matters into their own hands, learning how to speak more openly, and taking a route of greater independence. The treatment team must deal with the stress that emerges from giving the parents the right to choose who they want to work with. The one who is not chosen by the parents doesn't waver, showing instead a very stable and strong front. The trust between the family and the treatment team continues to build, and so does the family's desire to continue the treatment.

Lastly, we strongly feel that the treatment is effective not only in dealing with school absenteeism or family violence, but also in helping the family deal with such social structures as schools or neighbourhoods. We believe that the ideas or requests of the family members are important, and if an idea is determined to be in the child's best interests, we allow them to follow through on it. We find that honouring such requests tends to help improve the progress of the treatment.

In summary, we look at the family's problem as a chance to provide a desperate family with a temporary refuge from their troubles, by giving them a chance to talk out their problems. It is then that they notice the true nature of their problems. They talk about them, think about them, and suffer a little more, searching for the answer as to how a true family should function. We believe our treatment method helps them to grow to be more independent, and helps them to help themselves.

In regard to how effective this treatment really is, we are still in the midst of further investigation. However, according to evidence from the many and various cases we have applied the treatment to, we believe our method can solve not only family violence problems, but can help provide insight into other psychological barriers the patient and his family may possess. We believe our method can provide professionals in mental health services with a new perspective on the treatment of such problems.

REFERENCES

AOYAMA, M. et al (1979) Relationship Between School Refusal and Violence *Psychiatrica et Neurologia Paediatrica Japonica* **19**:17-22.

ASHIKAGA, S. (1980) *A Document: Family Violence* Tokyo:Aki Shobo.

BROADWIN, I.T. (1932) A Contribution to the Study of Truancy *American Journal of Orthopsychiatry* **2**:253-259.

Bureau for Adolescent Problems in the Prime Minister's Office (1982) *White Paper on the Adolescent ,1981 edition* Tokyo: The Ministry of Finance Printing Office.

Bureau for Adolescent Problems in the Prime Minister's Office (1984) *White Paper on the Adolescent ,1983 edition* Tokyo: The Ministry of Finance Printing Office.

Bureau for Adolescent Problems in the Prime Minister's Office (1985) *White Paper on the Adolescent, 1984 edition* Tokyo: The Ministry of Finance Printing Office.

Bureau for Adolescent Problems in the Prime Minister's Office (1986) *White Paper on the Adolescent, 1985 edition* Tokyo: The Ministry of Finance Printing Office.

COOLIDGE, J.C.; HAHN, P.B. & PECK, A.L. (1957) School Phobia, Neurotic Crisis or Way of Life: in Workshop "School Phobia" *American Journal of Orthopsychiatry* **27**:296.

COOLIDGE, J.C., WILLER, M.L.; TESSMAN, E. & WALDFOGEL, S. (1959) School Phobia in Adolescence: A Manifestation of Severe Character Disturbance *American Journal of Orthopsychiatry* **29**:599-607.

DOI, T. (1973) *The Anatomy of Dependence* Tokyo: Kodansha International.

DOI, T. (1977) *Interview as a Method: Help for Clinicians* Tokyo: Igaku Shoin.

EBATA, R. & TAKAHASHI, Y. (1978) Family Violence: Symptoms, Background, and Therapy *Seitoshido* **8**:6-19.

Economic Planning Agency (1983) *White Paper on the Living Conditions of the Japanese Nation, 1983 Edition* Tokyo: The Ministry of Finance Printing Office.

EISENBERG, L. (1958) School Phobia: A Study in the Communication of Anxiety *American Journal of Psychiatry* **114**:712-718.

ERIKSON, E.H. (1959) *Identity and the Life Cycle: Selected Papers in Psychological Issues* New York: International University Press.

Family Court Research Association on Current Problems of Juvenile Delinquency (1979) *Juvenile Delinquency in Japan: The Characteristics and Analysis of the Third Rise in Juvenile Delinquency* Tokyo: Taisei Shuppansha.

HERBERT, M. (1978) *Conduct Disorders of Childhood and Adolescence (A Behavioural Approach to Assessment and Treatment)* New York: John Wiley & Sons.

HERSOV, L.A. (1960) Persistent Non-Attendance at School *Child Psychology and Psychiatry* **1**:130-136.

HERSOV, L.A. (1960) Refusal to go to School *Child Psychology and Psychiatry*
1:137-145.

HONJO, S. (1983) The Characteristics of School-Skipping Children Who Commit
Family Violence *Japanese Journal of Child and Adolescent Psychiatry*
24,5:337-353.

INAMURA, H. (1980) *Family Violence: Pathology of the Typical Japanese Parent-
Child Relationship* Tokyo: Shin-yo-sha.

INAMURA, H. (1981) Family Violence and School Refusal *Kyoikushinri*
29:362-365.

ISHIKAWA, Y. & AOKI, S. (1982) Juvenile Delinquency. In: K. Baba (ed.)
Psychotherapy for Adolescence Tokyo: Kongo Shuppan.

ISHIKAWA, Y. & AOKI, S. (1985) Psychotherapy of Violent Aggressiveness. In: K.
Baba (ed.) *Analysis of Japanese Depth-Mentality, Volume 4* Tokyo: Yuhikaku.

ISHIKAWA, Y. & AOKI, S. (1986) *Adolescent Crisis and the Family: Therapy of
School Refusal and Family Violence by Team Treatment* Tokyo: Iwasaki
Gakujutsu Shuppansha.

ISHIKAWA, Y. (1988) School Refusal with Juvenile Delinquency. In: M. Asai (ed.)
Practical Lectures on Mental Health, Volume 4 Tokyo: Japan Library Centre.

IWAI, H. (1980) Family Violence and Family Pathology *Japanese Journal of
Psychotherapy* **6**,3:217-225.

JACKSON, L. (1964) Anxiety in Adolescents in Relation to School Refusal *Journal
of Child Psychiatry* **5**:59-73.

JOHNSON, A.M.; FALSTEIN, E.I.; SZUREK, S.A. & SVENDSEN, M. (1941) School Phobia
American Journal of Orthopsychiatry **11**:702-711.

KAHN, J.H. & NURSTEN, J.P. (1962) School Refusal: A Comprehensive View of
Shool Phobia and Other Failures of School Attendance *American Journal of
Orthopsychiatry* **32**:707-718.

KAWAI, H. (1976) *Japan as a Maternal Society and its Pathology* Tokyo:
Chuo-koron-sha.

MAKITA, K. (1967) Clinical Research on Truant Children in their Puberty:
Focusing on Serious Chronic Cases *Japanese Journal of Child and Adolescent
Psychiatry* **8**,4:377-384.

MASTERSON, J.F. (1972) *The Treatment of the Borderline Adolescent: A
Developmental Approach* New York: John Wiley & Sons.

MESSER, A.A. (1964) Family Treatment of a School Phobic Child *Archives of
General Psychiatry* **11**:548-555.

MIHARA, R. (1983) Relationship Between School Refusal and Family Violence *Japanese Journal of Clinical Psychiatry* **12**,7:915-922.

MURASE, K. (1980) Family Violence. In: T. Uriu (ed.) *School Violence and Family Violence* Tokyo: Yuhikaku.

PARTRIDGE, J.M. (1939) Truancy *Journal of Mental Science* **85**:45-81.

Police Force (1981) *White Paper on the Police, 1981 edition* Tokyo: The Ministry of Finance Printing Office.

Police Force (1985) *White Paper on the Police, 1985 Edition* Tokyo: The Ministry of Finance Printing Office.

SATO, T. & USUI, H. (1981) Clinical Research on Family Violence by the Adolescent *Japanese Journal of Psychotherapy* **7**,4:352-362.

SHIMIZU, M. (1979) *Family Violence: A Pitfall in Child Rearing from a Psychiatrist's Point of View* Tokyo: Toki Shobo.

SKYNNER, A.C.R. (1967) School Phobia: A Reappraisal *British Journal of Medical Psychology* **47**:1-16.

STORR, A. (1968) *Human Aggression* Middlesex: Penguin Press.

SUTTENFIELD, V. (1954) School Phobia: A Study of Five Cases *American Journal of Orthopsychiatry* **24**:368-380.

TAKAGI, R. (1963) Mental Mechanisms of School Phobia and its Prevention *Acta Paedopsychiatrica* **30**:135-140.

TAKAGI, R. (1972) The Family Structure of School Phobias *Acta Paedopsychiatrica* **38**:131-146.

TAKAHASHI, Y. (1979) Family Violence by the Adolescent *Japanese Journal of Clinical Psychiatry* **8**,8:917-922.

TALBOT, M. (1957) Panic in School Phobia *American Journal of Orthopsychiatry* **27**:286-295.

UCHIYAMA, K. (1983) Family Violence and School Refusal. In: K. Uchiyama (ed.) *School Refusal* Tokyo: Kongo Shuppan.

URIU, T. (1980) Loss and Recovery of Paternity. In: T. Uriu (ed.) *School Violence and Family Violence* Tokyo: Yuhikaku.

WAKABAYASHI, S. (1982) Clinical Research on Family Violence *Annual Report by Yasuda Life Welfare Foundation* **18**:127-136.

WAKABAYASHI, S. & HONJO, S. (1987) *Family Violence* Tokyo: Kongo Shuppan.

WARREN, W. (1948) Acute Neurotic Breakdown in Children with Refusal to go to School *Archives of Disturbed Childhood* **18**:266-272.

Difference Between Crisis and Trauma: Consequences for Intervention

Berthold P.R. Gersons

Introduction

In the 1960's, Gerald Caplan and others introduced the concept of crisis as a time-limited disruption to the normal steady state of an individual. It became quite a popular and also optimistic concept during those years because it proposed that the development of psychiatric disorders could be prevented by crisis intervention. The crisis-paradigm became the basis worldwide for a reshaping of mental health services, formulated within the strategies of public mental health care. The crisis-approach embodied the ideals of the community mental health movements: the large-scale battle against stigmatization and the exclusion of the mentally ill from mainstream society. Caplan's book "The Principles of Preventive Psychiatry" (1964) became the handbook for this worldwide campaign to prevent mental illness.

In the Netherlands the crisis-concept was received with great enthusiasm. There was a striking similarity between the approach and prevention of hospital admission by the use of outreach psychiatric emergency services, already started in the 1930's by the Dutch community psychiatrist Querido. In the '70's, crisis intervention centres came into being and were supplemented by the application of mental health consultation.

Nowadays we still consider the concept of crisis intervention to be very useful, but in the Netherlands we have to admit that these centres and services, which were based on those promising public health targets, seem to serve primarily those who are already the victims of long-standing chronic mental illness. Crisis intervention services - with the aim of preventing mental illness - have come into existence again under new names, with less broadly formulated targets devoted to preventing what is called post-traumatic stress reaction - for example, crime-victim's aid, intervention in family violence and child abuse, and post-disaster briefing.

Therefore, in this paper, with respect to the mentioned background of recent developments, I will firstly elaborate the concept of crisis, its consequences for crisis intervention, and then present its evolution towards the concept of trauma. I will close by drawing conclusions regarding the consequences for mental health care delivery.

Crisis theory

Two community psychiatrists trained in psychoanalysis, Erich Lindemann and Gerald Caplan, developed crisis theory and crisis intervention on the basis of their experiences with grief and mourning. Lindemann's (1944) classic article on the "Symptomatology and Management of Acute Grief" was the first description after Freud's seminal work "Mourning and Melancholia" of the process of mourning. It was based on his clinical work with the victims of the Coconut Grove night club fire in Boston in 1944, a disaster in which 500 persons perished. He observed that people not previously thought to suffer from mental illness could develop psychopathological symptoms after experiencing severe loss. This observation was of the utmost importance in that it surpassed the generally accepted sharp boundary between mental health and mental illness. The paper presents not only a very clear description of signs and symptoms of bereavement, but also delineates the development of mourning as a process in time and of its ultimate resolution. At the time of Lindemann's writing, with the exception of psychoanalytic theories, there was little understanding of the developmental processes underlying mental illness.

I would therefore like to quote some of Lindemann's pioneering statements:

1. Acute grief is a definite syndrome with psychological and somatic symptomatology;
2. This syndrome may appear immediately after a crisis, or it may be delayed; it may be exaggerated or apparently absent;
3. In place of the typical syndrome, there may appear distorted pictures, each of which represents one special aspect of the grief syndrome;
4. By appropriate techniques these distorted pictures can be successfully transformed into a normal grief reaction with resolution.

So it seems every reaction was possible - a broad spectrum of trauma responses, so to speak - and yet it was not seen as too complicated to apply therapy with success.

From this description it is clear that Lindemann was already struggling to draw a line between a normal reaction and pathology. Lindemann called it therefore "the symptomatology of *normal* grief": somatic distress, preoccupation with the image of the deceased, guilt, hostile reactions, and loss of patterns of conduct: all symptoms which he called "pathognomic" for grief, yet with the application of "appropriate techniques" symptoms which could easily be resolved.

In Lindemann's article, the word "crisis" is used without any further explanation. Caplan (1964) later defines crisis very simply (and without much attention to psychopathological phenomena) as "an upset in a steady state". He further distinguishes four levels of severity of crisis reactions, of which the highest level is a psychotic reaction. There is no sharp boundary any more between normality and pathology.

The definitions of crisis have always been very broadly formulated. Crisis has mostly been conceptualised as a limited period of disorganisation of normal mental functioning. However, with such a broad formulation in mind, one must ask questions such as which cases are crises? at what moments do crises occur? how should crisis intervention be delivered? Crisis intervention is mostly described as a time-limited form of psychotherapy, focused on catharsis and on problem solving.

As already said, when one reads the above-mentioned and other articles on crisis theory and intervention, one is struck by the optimism regarding the outcome of crisis situations. It is interesting to consider that these optimistic notions were heavily influenced by the war and postwar experiences. In World War I shellshock was found to be a widespread phenomenon which destroyed, temporarily or indefinitely, the mental life of thousands of soldiers in the trenches. Consequently, in Word War II a million men were not allowed to enter military service because of mental disabilities. The high prevalence rates of mental illness found in military screening, and also in large scale population-surveys, fostered after the second World War a strong public concern with mental illness. This became the substratum for a worldwide public mental health campaign. However, in my opinion the high prevalence rate of mental disorder paradoxically served to further the belief that mental illness was **not** a widespread phenomenon. To explain this contradiction one has to consider that two types of mental illness were thought to occur: the so-called "minor reactions" to the stresses of war and of living in society, and the major mental illnesses such as schizophrenia. The concept of crisis intervention fitted well with this optimistic and idealistic belief that whilst the former were widespread, relatively few people suffered from long-standing psychiatric illness.

In the development of crisis theory the attention of investigators and clinicians has as a consequence moved much more towards factors which were supposed to be essential in the crisis process. Questions such as: which life-events are important causes of crises? how can the magnitude of a stressor be measured? became important in research and crisis literature. An example of such early investigation into the crisis process is the pioneering work of Tyhurst (1951). He was interested in individual reactions to community disasters, for example shipwreck and fire, but also in minor events, such as moving house. He distinguished three phases in the crisis process:

- the *impact phase*, which is the period of danger or threat;
- the *recoil phase*, the period immediately after the danger has stopped;
- and last the *post-traumatic phase,* which is the route back to the steady state of normal life.

In the impact phase the individual reacts mostly instrumentally without being bothered by strong emotions. All actions are taken to either reach safety or to fight the danger. If no action is undertaken, the person will stay in a sometimes dangerous state of disbelief and denial, which is called "psychogenic death". The person's cognitive orientation in time is focused very sharply on the immediate "here and now". (It is always striking to find, months or years later, how sharp and precise the memories regarding the experiences in the impact phase still are.)

The recoil phase is characterised by a dramatic change. There is no need any more for immediate action. Now the catharsis of emotions stands in the foreground. Denial or outrage and crying are prominent; strong exhaustion may also be felt. The cognitive orientation in time is now focused on the immediate past. There exists no interest in the future, nor in the further past. Later on, the memory of this phase is usually not at all precise.

In the post-traumatic phase the person tries to integrate the distressing experience within their life history in order to give it a personal meaning.

Tyhurst has outlined both a sequence of psychological phenomena experienced as emotions, and the element of time-perspective orientation in cognitive functioning - thus clarifying a kind of spiral one has to go through in order to work through the bad experience. He has called these "transitional states" (the impact, recoil and post traumatic phases), which a person has to go through in the crisis process. In this spiral there is an alternation of cognitive functioning and emotional abreaction. Others, such as Klein & Lindemann (1961) have contributed another important notion for the understanding of the crisis process from a social-psychological perspective: the change in roles which one experiences through these phases in a crisis. The role concept is related to the feeling of control over what is expected of one by others in any given situation; for example, being a friend is very different from being a teacher. So, as an illustration, at the beginning of a crisis one can be, say, a tourist in an hotel; later on a possible victim of a fire; then again the survivor; later, a patient in hospital; or a bereaved relative, etc. This sequence of different roles faces the individual with different adaptive tasks and therefore places stress upon his coping repertoire. Also, and this is perhaps crucial in the development of post-traumatic stress disorder, one is confronted with one's own vulnerability and loss of control.

To summarise, the starting points of crisis intervention thus far are:
1. Crisis is a temporary experience, a time-limited process of days or weeks;
2. Crises develop within a network of committed persons;
3. Help and support will be delivered by involved persons from the immediate network;
4. Psychiatric symptoms in a state of crisis are mostly of a temporary nature and relate directly to the crisis;
5. A minimum of help and support is sufficient for a maximum effect.

Homeostasis

Crisis theory has been heavily influenced by the optimistic notions derived from physiology regarding homeostasis and adaptation to stress. This is quite understandable. How do we explain that we can walk freely, talk and read without having to constantly control our bodily functions? This is possible because of what Walter Cannon (1932) has called the homeostasis of bodily functions, the need to maintain a constant equilibrium. Influences from the outside world are usually counteracted by autonomic physiological reactions, as for example perspiration in a hot room, but also through cognitive awareness of feeling too warm and consequently taking off a sweater. Homeostasis is similar to some kind of "automatic pilot". Cannon also postulated the principle of homeostasis for psychological and social processes.

Lindemann has clearly taken these concepts on board when he speaks of the "emotional disequilibrium" in crisis. "In a crisis situation … a special meaning of the environmental circumstances upsets the structuring of intrapsychic forces. During the period there may be a realignment of forces and this will lead to a new state of equilibrium which often differs from the former".

Therefore, crisis is conceptualised by Lindemann and others (1956; 1961) as a temporary threat towards the psychosocial homeostasis. As a consequence, crisis intervention has been described in terms of forces and equilibrium. The actions to be undertaken are:

- altering the balance of forces;
- restoration of a reasonably healthy equilibrium in a social orbit;
- repopulating the social space;
- redistribution of role relationships within the group.

All action is counteraction, undertaken to restore the psychosocial homeostasis.

However, much less consideration was given to outcomes if homeostasis failed. Could only death follow? Here we have to mention the work of Hans Selye (1964), who conceptualised the "General Adaptation Syndrome". By this he meant the responses of the body to major stress, passing through the alarm reaction to resistance and finally into exhaustion. Many similarities can be seen between Selye's description of the General Adaption Syndrome and the psychological phases outlined by Tyhurst. Even more important is Selye's concept of *heterostatis*, by which he meant an *abnormal equilibrium* which has been established against potential "pathogens" from the outside. Essential to this concept of heterostasis is the notion that such a physiological and psychological defence-state manifests without any external threat of danger.

To make it even more clear: whilst we speak of crisis as a time-limited state of disequilibrium, in heterostasis there is no clear expectation as to either the end of it or the outcome. The familiar pattern of psychological phenomena following the experience of a trauma is seen as a normal reaction and as a state of disequilibrium. If such a crisis is not resolved within a given period, a state of heterostasis evolves as a new abnormal equilibrium which is nowadays often referred to as Post-Traumatic Stress Disorder.

Lindemann also distinguished "distorted and maladaptive grief reactions" such as (1) overactivity without a sense of loss; (2) symptoms belonging to the last illness of the deceased; (3) conversion symptoms; (4) social isolation; (5) overflowing hostility against others; (6) absence of emotional display; (7) lasting loss of patterns of social interaction; (8) bringing detrimental activities to one's own social and economic existence; and (9) even agitated depression. These are signs of a new pathological equilibrium.

Trauma and transition

Now we come to the concept of trauma. From a traditional psychoanalytic viewpoint, trauma is generally considered to be a past, bad, childhood experience which has been put away into the unconscious. By use of psychotherapy such a trauma can be brought back to the surface of conscious mental functioning, where it will lose its disruptive influence on functioning. As part of the research into the causation of depression, researchers such as Brown and Harris (1978) have studied the "traumatic capacity" of life events.

There is much discussion as to what makes life events causative factors of mental breakdown. Psychoanalysts favour the viewpoint that life-events can become active destroyers of mental functioning because of their unconscious meaning. From this perspective, the life-event coincides with a past "forgotten" traumatic event.

However, within the research into Post-Traumatic Stress Disorder (PTSD) negative life-events are considered to be actual destroyers of mental functioning because of their traumatic magnitude. Krystal (1978) formulates this as follows: "Trauma involves the overwhelming of the normal self-preserving functions in the face of inevitable danger. The recognition of the existence of unavoidable danger and the surrender to it marks the onset of traumatic state, and with it, the... traumatic process which, if uninterrupted, terminates in psychogenic death". The traumatic process is described by him as first "a paralysed overwhelmed state with immobilisation, withdrawal, possible depersonalisation and evidence of disorganisation. There may be a regression in any and all spheres and aspects of mental function and affect expression. This regression is followed by characteristic recuperative attempts through repetition, typical dreams and eventually by long-term neurotic, characterological, psychosomatic or other syndromes".

Post-Traumatic Stress Disorder, therefore, represents the sequelae of recent traumatic life-events, but also demonstrates the gross stress it has brought about in the individual. Thus, PTSD can be described as a state of heterostasis, an abnormal equilibrium, and not just an unsuccessful mastery of stress; it is this heterostasis which is seen as the target of crisis intervention (Caplan, 1981). PTSD is a transitional state and yet there is an inability to proceed to the next stage and thus end the transitional process.

Our arguments are based on our research and experience with PTSD in the police force (Gersons, 1989). We learned of police officers who, having participated for instance in shooting incidents, were left in a state of crisis. This is an accepted phenomenon within the police force. However, later on, when the incident has been forgotten by fellow police officers, the involved officer still struggles with the traumatic experience, with such struggle often going unrecognised by others. It is still unknown as to whether rapid crisis intervention (such as debriefing) in such situations can really be effective in preventing the longer sequelae of PTSD.

So, in relation to trauma within the conceptualisation of Post-Traumatic Stress Disorders, crisis intervention is faced with the following questions:

1. Is it possible to prevent the development of PTSD?
2. If so, what can organisations such as the police force do to prevent PTSD?
3. When and where does the need to treat PTSD by mental health professionals begin?

Consequences for intervention

We now come to the consequences for intervention. We have argued that the concept of crisis relates to a sudden disruption in the steady state of psychosocial functioning of an individual or family. The strategies of crisis intervention are aimed at restoring a satisfactory equilibrium within a short period. In the middle of this century, it was expected that crisis intervention could not only help to restore a person's steady state but could also help to prevent the development of mental illness. Nowadays however, crisis intervention services, as demonstrated by writers such as Hoult (1984) and Stein (1975), still have as a goal the restoration of an acceptable equilibrium in a person's situation, but primarily serve those with long-standing mental illness. It is also clear from our Dutch experiences that the chronic mentally ill are highly vulnerable to even minor events and therefore are much more in need of crisis intervention services on a regular basis than is the general population. Yet still within crisis intervention strategies psychopathological phenomena are given limited importance and are judged as context-variables which to a certain extent can complicate crisis intervention procedures. Restoration of normal functioning of chronic patients and thus including them in mainstream society as much as possible still remains the high ideal of crisis intervention.

We have to acknowledge that we are not so sure about the power of crisis intervention in preventing temporary or more long-standing disturbances of psychosocial functioning in persons who do not suffer from major mental illness. There is no question about the humanitarian value of supporting persons in great distress. However, we are not certain what, if anything, such efforts will prevent in the long run. We have to recognise that both social support and professional crisis intervention can be helpful for perhaps many victims of traumatic life events but not for all. Surely, crisis intervention has to be followed up by professional therapeutic services; otherwise the state of heterostasis, as in PTSD, may not, in the long run, be resolved. Trauma is not a minor event in human life; rather, it can destroy much of what has been previously safeguarded in the psychosocial development of the human being. We know this from rape victims, incest victims, the Holocaust, and also from victims of disasters such as fire or flood. To suggest that crisis intervention is sufficient is too idealistic an attitude and does not take into account the after-effects of overwhelming events.

REFERENCES

BRESLAU, N. & DAVIS, G.C. (1987) Post-Traumatic Stress Disorder: The Stressor Criterion *Journal of Nervous and Mental Disease* **175**:5, 255-264.

BROWN, G.W. & HARRIS, T. (1978) *Social Origins of Depression: A Study of Psychiatric Disorder in Women* London: Tavistock Publications.

CANNON, W. (1939) *The Wisdom of the Body* New York: Norton.

CAPLAN, G. (1964) *Principles of Preventive Psychiatry* New York: Basic Books.

CAPLAN, G. (1981) Mastery of Stress: Psychosocial Aspects *American Journal of Psychiatry* **138**,4:413-420.

GERSONS, B.P.R. (1989) Patterns of PTSD Among Police Officers Following Shooting Incidents: A Two-Dimensional Model and Treatment Implications *Journal of Traumatic Stress* **2**,3:247-258.

HOULT, J. & REYNOLDS, I. (1984) Schizophrenia: A Comparative Trial of Community Oriented and Hospital Oriented Psychiatric Care *Acta Psychiatrica Scandanavica* **69**:359-373

KLEIN, D.C. & LINDEMANN, E. (1961). Preventive Intervention in Individual and Family Crisis Situations. In: G. Caplan (ed.) *Prevention of Mental Disorders in Children* New York: Basic Books.

KRYSTAL, H. (1981) Trauma and Affects *Psychoanalytic Study of the Child* **33**:81-116.

LINDEMANN, E. (1944) The Symptomatology and Management of Acute Grief *American Journal of Psychiatry* **10**:141-148.

LINDEMANN, E. (1956) The Meaning of Crisis in Individual and Family Living *Teaching College Rec* **57**:310-315.

SELYE, H. (1964) *From Dream to Discovery: On Being a Scientist* New York: McGraw Hill.

STEIN, L.I.; TEST, M.A. & MARX, A.J. (1975) Alternative to the Hospital: A Controlled Study *American Journal of Psychiatry* **132**:517-522

TYHURST, J.S. (1957) The Role of Transition States - Including Disasters in Mental Illness. In: *Symposium on Preventive and Social Psychiatry* Washington D.C.: Walter Reed Army Institute of Research.

The Disaster Response Cycle

Rachel Rosser & Gary Jackson

Introduction

Clinical disciplines develop in series of cycles. Starting with and from the patient, we listen intently, gather information, construe it to generate hypotheses which we then put to the test in interventions. We return to the patient, learn from what we have done, and go on, cycling forward in progressive spirals, from the patient, back to the patient.

We have come through many turns in learning about the effects of extraordinary stressful events. Much has changed, both in the way that mental health professionals understand the issues and in the way that other fields and the general public view them. When one of us co-authored a review of the literature on disaster psychiatry (Kinston & Rosser, 1974), many requests for reprints of the article were made. However, people refused to believe that psychiatric interventions may be required in "ordinary" everyday types of disasters. The literature up until then had focused on Hiroshima, Nagasaki, the Holocaust and the Vietnam war and was consequently suspected of being inapplicable to other types of disasters. Research and practice over the last 15 years have shown this clearly not to be the case. Dealing with victims of the King's Cross fire, the Lockerbie air disaster, the sinking of the Marchioness cruise boat in the Thames and many other disasters, as well as domestic and personal disasters, we have confirmed common characteristics in their effects on mental health.

The issues which currently constitute the learning-acting cycle of the psychiatry of the disaster response syndromes are numerous. They encompass phenomenology, taxonomy, medical therapeutics, psychosocial interventions, the logistics of service provision and the law. Each cycle has two phases. The first, which immediately follows the disaster, involves saving life, dealing with major physical injury and preliminary mental health relief measures, such as psychological debriefing (Dyregrov, 1989). The second phase involves comprehensive psychiatric assessment, providing treatment services (psychological, physical, psychosocial), active follow up, treatment evaluation and consultation on health education and legal developments. This process leads back to service planning so that all that has been learned is used in responding to the needs of the victims of the next disaster. Phase two is necessarily a long-term exercise. We call this phasic process the Disaster Response Cycle.

Phenomenology and taxonomy

Through study of the psychological responses to disasters, a distinction can be drawn between the primary, and secondary and associated, phenomena. The most characteristic phenomenon is re-experiencing the mental state which existed at the time of the disaster, or in the aftermath. This includes disturbing dreams, abnormal perceptions, and obsessional and compulsive phenomena, often accompanied by intense emotion. Abnormal perceptions include perceptual distortions, so that a cupboard door is opened and instead of catching a coat which falls out, you are catching a body. Even more alarming are hallucinations, which are almost universal in victims and in the past have been grossly underestimated. The reason why they have been grossly underestimated is that people feel that they are going crazy. They are loathe to, and have few ways to, articulate this; much time can go by before, with gentle probing, they are able to define what they are experiencing. Victims of the King's Cross fire have described the recurrence of the smell of burning flesh; similarly, Marchioness survivors have described falling over in the corridor at work as it suddenly begins to sway. Auditory and tactile perceptual distortions and deceptions are very common. Those survivors who retain some control are, in a way, more fortunate; the form then is of obsessional thoughts which they try to resist, using a great deal of mental energy.

The secondary phenomena include generalised anxiety, phobias, panics, hypervigilence and agitation. Stimuli to which victims develop phobias may generalise, so that not only does a King's Cross survivor avoid the underground, but any public transport or place out of which rapid escape would be difficult. Of associated insomnias, interrupted sleep and early waking are the most common. One Marchioness survivor, aged only 22, will soon have to have all of his teeth capped as he has ground them away in his sleep. A King's Cross survivor gets up in the night and wanders around the streets, in a dissociated state. Behavioural changes occur, so that triggering experiences are avoided. There may be an enormous increase in risk taking, such as drinking excessive alcohol, drunk driving, speeding, other substance abuse, and overspending.

There are other frequently encountered symptoms which have however been dropped from the operational diagnostic criteria of DSM-III-R and ICD 10 (Diagnostic & Statistical Manual, Third Edition (Revised) 1987; International Classification of Diseases, 1989). Survivor guilt was vividly described by Lifton (1967) after Hiroshima. Depersonalisation is common and is often a defence against survivor guilt. Tremendous anger is seen in victims of both man-made and natural disasters. The euphoria of the Hero syndrome almost invariably occurs in at least one victim of each disaster. It is usually followed by a period of severe depression.

The ramifications of having these problems are that victims can no longer function as a parent, a spouse or a worker. Some victims go into overdrive, dedicating all of their time to work, or, for example, disaster fund raising, which leads to neglect and disintegration of their personal life.

Having registered the phenomenology, we have to aggregate and classify it. We choose at present, by convention, to talk about Post-Traumatic Stress Disorder (PTSD) (DSM-III-R). However, it would seem. from the variety of the phenomena, more appropriate to talk of the Post-

Traumatic Stress Disorders. One example of the need for this is that we can cope with acute, delayed and chronic, within our classification system, but we consistently miss a recurrent Post-Traumatic Stress Disorder category. One of our Marchioness survivors had an episode of PTSD, lasting for three years, in his adolescence and then a second episode following the boat experience, which was made more severe by the addition of exhumed material related to his first episode. We are becoming more convinced of a notion of acute-on-chronic traumatic stress, culminating in a full post-traumatic stress syndrome, following a sufficient, last-straw stressor.

The taxonomy of these syndromes is made more difficult by the psychotic phenomena which are so commonly part of the clinical presentation. Mention has been made of the hallucinations which may recur constantly during protracted re-experiencing episodes, lasting up to thirty minutes. These patients do not have the "advantage" of losing insight, as in the major psychoses; this must severely increase the distress caused by the experiences.

Service provision

Whilst creating a taxonomy for the clinical syndromes, we also have to address the logistical issues of patient identification in what is often a chaotic post-disaster environment. Most of the need is not, at least initially, overt, and one has to inform people of potential reactions so that they can identify their own need. "Victims" should be seen to include survivors, relatives, helpers and witnesses. Victims need to be screened for severity and prioritised for allocation to sources of psychological and social expertise. An outreach for the majority who do not come forward spontaneously requires a programme commitment of three or more years. Particularly difficult times, during which relapses may occur, are at inquests and during official enquiries, and on the first and even subsequent anniversaries.

Response plans have to be locally determined so as to harness local resources, although at certain times it will be necessary to consult or bring in experts from the outside. If possible, it is important to establish a multidisciplinary steering group. This should have a designated chair, so as to avoid the problems of leadership vacuum or conflict, which can complicate emergency responses.

There is a great need for professionals to collaborate with the media. We can become advocates for the survivors and bereaved relatives in this way. The media can be extremely helpful in getting out information and powerfully supporting just causes. However, the nature of the issues involved, not least the disaster itself, demands concerted, even high profile, but delicate, medical media handling. Sensationalism is an outcome to be avoided.

The next clinical task (after patient recognition and the classification of the phenomenology) in phase two, is the provision of specific

131

psychosocial interventions. A wide range of treatments has been employed by workers in this field, although little has been written about them, and even less about evaluation of them. We, at the UCMSM Academic Department of Psychiatry are, after much discussion of ethical and logistic issues, undertaking trials of psychotherapy for the Post-Traumatic Stress Disorders. Initially, we set up a waiting list, single blind controlled trial, into which we entered sixty patients from major disasters. We are currently (1990) carrying out the one year follow-up of this group and hope to publish our findings before too long.

We have recently embarked on a randomised single blind controlled trial (double blind conditions are not possible with psychological treatments). In this trial we compare intensive psychological debriefing with and without subsequent therapy sessions. This involves six to seven hours of assessment and then three to four hours of debriefing, followed in a randomised half of the sample by a series of psychotherapeutic sessions. We are incorporating quality of life measures which we regard as particularly important. We also have an economist involved so that we can work on cost utility analyses. We already have convincing statistical evidence that there is benefit from the psychotherapy, but that interestingly there may also be a place for a waiting period; a period when you know that you are going to have therapy, but you make adjustments in the interim. We find that those who wait for a while are somewhat improved on measures of social adjustment but may suffer a reactive disruption in their relationships early on in therapy (Rosser, Dewar & Thompson - in print).

At present we are exploring the limits of psychosocial interventions. In the more chronic cases, however, the imprint on the personality may be so biologically engrained, that only long-term psychotropic medication and other physical interventions may be efficacious, notwithstanding their impact on complex servo mechanisms and on cerebral lateralisation.

Policy development

As specialist clinicians, we have a responsibility to contribute to response planning at all levels. Our team invites representatives from Whitehall, the Home Office and the Law to researchers' meetings, so that expertise is made available to these important policy makers. Our collaboration with the Law also involves preparing legal reports for clients who are pursuing compensation claims, and in helping establish legal precedents, as expert witnesses. A case history will therefore be presented in some detail below. This case demonstrates a new aspect to Post-traumatic Stress Disorder and the establishment of a legal precedent in this field. It is thus an example of the progress being made through the ever-developing cycles of responding to the needs of disaster victims.

On the night of the King's Cross fire, a young ambulance driver, Raymond Parker, was called back just as he was going off duty, and told to help the emergency crew. He had no experience of a major disaster and had not been briefed. He opened the back door of an ambulance which had arrived at the casualty department and was confronted with severely burned survivors. Two years later, he committed a crime; he went to court five times and on each occasion the case was adjourned. There had been some psychological assessment but not with the orientation which was really needed. Eventually, through the legal aid system, he came under the care of one of our most experienced barristers, who is also a member of the House of Commons, and he referred Raymond to one of the authors (RR). Raymond was experiencing florid Post-Traumatic Stress Disorder. He had been driving around London with his head out of the window, trying to get rid of the smell of burned flesh. He had so overworked as a coping strategy, that he had neglected his family to the point that he failed to give his pregnant girlfriend a lift one night, and she was killed by a taxi as she tried to hail it down. He went on furiously overworking until he broke down. When he was seen in our department eighteen months after the King's Cross fire, he was experiencing panic attacks and intrusive recollections of the event when he tried to travel on the underground. He was tearful and depressed and described repeated olfactory hallucinations.

In the early history it was relevant that his mother was grieving for the loss of her first-born son who died from cot death, during the second half of her pregnancy with Raymond. Raymond grew up with some knowledge of his brother's death. The youngest child, born four years after Raymond, had a severe congenital deformity which required almost continuous in-patient treatment for the first six years of his life. Raymond spent much time in his early childhood at the hospital and consequently developed a strong fear of hospitals which he only began to overcome as an ambulanceman. His father, who he recalled as a somewhat aggressive giant, had a leg amputated and two years later, when Raymond was six, died, leaving his wife with no source of income and four children under seven years old. Because of the effect of these multiple losses on herself, Mrs. Parker was more unlikely to be able to fulfil Raymond's emotional needs. His consequent deprivation, on top of his own experience of severe loss, inhibited the development of Raymond's emotional security.

He suffered a further traumatic loss of a significant person at the age of sixteen, when his favourite teacher, who was very important to him, died suddenly. Raymond began to study the subject which this teacher had taught and even took over his job at the school for a while. He passed his trade examinations well, but felt a vocation to help people. He thus joined the ambulance service. By this time then, he had experienced a life characterised by traumatic losses, the mourning of and adjustment to which were not facilitated and never completed, and were thus carried forward making him vulnerable to subsequent trauma.

The Crown Court received RR's evidence together with extracts from the official Fennell report and data from our research in the field. Raymond pleaded guilty and received a two year suspended prison sentence, on the understanding that he would attend our clinic as an out-patient. This sentence was much reduced from the usual for the crime. This is as a result of Post-Traumatic Stress Disorder having been accepted as an extenuating circumstance in a criminal action (The Guardian Newspaper, 1989; the Daily Telegraph Newspaper, 1989), and was the first case in the United Kingdom to establish this legal milestone.

The clinical notion which this case also establishes is the clear evidence for Raymond having been specifically vulnerable, after suffering multiple significant stressful life events, to developing PTSD after a critical event. He had grown up as driven, unable to relax, to realise the potential of himself alone or in relationships, or to experience pleasure. His vulnerabilities had begun to develop at the age of four.

In others, problems begin even earlier. Conversely, a prolonged dehumanising experience at a later stage can partially neutralise the early nurture of a good enough home environment and subsequent normal process of becoming a person. Bruno Bettelheim demonstrates this in his book "The Informed Heart" (1961).

We have learned much, and we hope that without having to cycle through many more disaster responses, we will be offering comprehensively informed interventions to our patients.

REFERENCES

American Psychiatric Association (1987) *Diagnostic and Statistical Manual, Third Edition (Revised)* Washington D.C.: American Psychiatric Association Press.

BETTELHEIM, B. (1961) *The Informed Heart* London: Thames & Hudson.

DYREGROV, A. (1989) Caring for Helpers in Disaster Situations: Psychological Debriefing *Disaster Management* **2**,1:25-30.

KINSTON, W. & ROSSER, R. (1974) Disaster: Effects on Mental and Physical State *Journal of Psychosomatic Research* **18**:427-456

LIFTON, R.J. (1967) *Death in Life:Survivors of Hiroshima* New York: Random House.

ROSSER, R.; DEWARS, S. & THOMPSON, J. (in print) The King's Cross Fire: Lecture to the Royal Society of Medicine *Journal of the Royal Society of Medicine*.

World Health Organisation (1989) *International Classification of Diseases* Geneva: World Health Organisation Press.

An Exceptional Course for an Exceptional Cause (1989) *The Guardian Newspaper* (Feb 8).

King's Cross Trauma Saves Man from Jail (1989) *The Daily Telegraph Newspaper* (Feb 19).

Providing Psychiatric Emergency Care During Disasters: Hurricane Hugo in Charleston, South Carolina.

Joseph J. Zealberg

> *The wise man in the storm prays God, not for safety*
> *from danger, but for deliverance from fear.*

> - Ralph Waldo Emerson

Hurricane Hugo

- The worst natural disaster in the U.S.A.

- Struck coast of South Carolina on September 21, 1989. Landfall winds exceeded 135mph (216Km/hr).

- Damage estimates are 6 billion dollars (approximately 3.5 billion pounds).

- Tidal surges exceeded 20ft (6 metres).

- By the time the storm passed, power and communications were down in 24 counties. 750,000 people were without power.

- 70% of the state's trees, enough to build 660,000 homes, were destroyed. Enough trees lost to rebuild Charleston 40 times.

- 29 people were killed despite massive evacuation.

- 65,000 homeless after the storm.

On September 21st, 1989 fear crept into the hearts of hundreds of thousands of Americans who lived on the southeastern coast of the United States, as Hurricane Hugo rapidly approached. The storm had formed a path of destruction as it crossed the Virgin Islands and Puerto Rico, leaving millions of dollars in damages as it continued its northwest journey toward the American mainland.

As the probability increased that the storm would affect Charleston, South Carolina, the members of our Emergency Psychiatry/Mobile Crisis Programme began planning for evacuation. This was a time of extraordinary tension and anxiety. The emergency team normally functions as the collaborative psychiatric emergency service for the Charleston Area Mental Health Centre (MHC) and the Medical University of South Carolina (MUSC), and as such, the programme's clinical staff was thoroughly experienced in dealing with severe psychiatric emergencies, both in emergency rooms and in the community at large. However, not one person who was alive in the Charleston area had ever witnessed a storm of equal intensity. The crisis team had been given the responsibility for co-ordinating emergency mental health disaster services for Charleston County, and this was to be their first experience in disaster.

On September 20th, the citizens of South Carolina's coastal areas were ordered to evacuate by government officials. We instructed our staff of clinicians to evacuate for safety and to contact us by beeper as soon as the storm passed. The emergency services programme manager (Jackie Puckett, A.C.S.W.) co-ordinated with civil defence authorities at the EOC (Emergency Operations Centre). The programme director (Joe Zealberg, M.D.) proceeded to a local school which had been converted to a hurricane shelter. Both of the programme's emergency automobiles were parked on high ground areas deemed to be safe and our emergency psychopharmacologic drug boxes and cellular telephones were locked away at the shelter. As time quickly passed, it became clear that landfall for Hurricane Hugo would be directly over Charleston.

No one was prepared to deal with the fury and awesome destructiveness of such a storm. Several hours before the storm arrived, the school principal at the shelter had gathered everyone together in order to give people an idea of what was to come. The shelter plan was designed to have lights out by a certain time that evening since it was readily apparent that a category IV storm would clearly knock out all utility power. People were instructed to prepare their flashlights ahead of time and to expect to hear an incredible amount of noise, wind, sounds of rushing, roaring, and sounds similar to "freight trains" all around the shelter. Volunteers from within the shelter were instructed to circulate throughout the shelter complex and constantly reassure people that things were fine, that after the noise and weather had blown over we would all be safe and that it was important to remain calm. Provisions were made to efficiently evacuate the shelter inhabitants from the first to the second floor, in the event of a storm surge flood.

As Hugo approached landfall, it became clear that the storm itself was actually larger than the entire state of South Carolina (which has an area of 30,207 square miles)! All television and radio communications were knocked out by the 135mph winds.

For those of us who stayed in the shelters, it appeared that our expertise in calming and supporting people was extremely useful. As the storm blew over, there was a strange and eerie silence within the shelter. The next morning one person said that she fantasised that the storm was the devil looking for victims. She said that she knew if she made any noise or if anyone in the room made any noise that he (the Devil) would know that we were within and he would break down the windows and doors and kill us. Numerous people used a similar metaphor and said that having the volunteers continue to come around and reassure them helped them through the night. During the eye of the storm, a young gentleman became acutely manic and tried to take control of the shelter's operations. Before panic could ensue, however, he was quickly reunited with his family and thereafter calmed down with support and limit setting.

As the storm passed, some six hours later, our disaster plan was initiated via telephone contact with the central EOC 100 miles away in Columbia, the state's capital. By that time, more than half of the state was without power, a situation which would last for weeks for many people.

By daylight the entire Charleston area had changed. Many areas had been flooded by the 19 foot tidal surge. Trees blocked sections of roads and cut through houses. Virtually every power line and pole was down. Where forests and woods once stood, broken stumps remained. Thousands of people were homeless. A few who disobeyed the evacuation order died. Thousands would have perished if the evacuation order had not been given. In one night's passing, the entire face of South Carolina had been altered.

Emotional phases surrounding Hugo

1. Anxiety, disbelief, denial, as storm travelled across ocean to S.E. coast.
2. Anxiety, tension, fear during evacuation.
3. Fear, anxiety and terror during the storm.
4. Awe, denial and rationalisation by many upon return (e.g. "at least we're alive").
5. Numbness, disbelief at destruction. Disorganisation due to loss of orientation cues.
6. Anger, difficulty with organising due to exhaustion, fatigue.
7. Shock at secondary-level injuries.
8. Some temporary disorganisation of chronically mentally ill. Responded quickly to support and treatments.
9. Stress reactions seen among helping professionals as needs of populace were met.
10. Influx of bipolars to "help Charleston repair".
11. Workers from other areas cause increase of substance abuse and homelessness.
12. Increase in suicide threats with firearms.
13. Slow resolution. Delayed onset of anxiety, depression and PTSD.
14. Anxiety rekindled at restart of hurricane season.

Few psychiatric emergencies were seen in the next two days. After witnessing Hugo's destructive power, most people were in a state of denial and shock, focusing on how glad they were to be alive. In the face of such massive destruction, things which people felt were most dear to them (i.e., material possessions, belongings and personal property) suddenly became of less importance. People were looking to basics (i.e. "Am I alive?" "Do I have food?" "Do I have water?"). A return to those basic needs allowed people to more comfortably deal with the immediate trauma of loss and this worked in a rather marvellous way to allow people to deal with their immediate needs and feel that they were "fortunate" compared to others who were less so. For example, people would say "I have only lost my house but the guy up the street lost his house and his boat and his car. I guess I'm really lucky." This change in perspective helped people through incredible traumas which otherwise would have consumed their psychological state of well being. Many others felt an immediate sense of survival guilt, especially those who were less affected by the storm and those people, in turn, were able to share their good fortune with others, thus diminishing any psychological disequilibrium.

People in the helping professions quickly learned that they needed to mobilise their services to help the community at large. Institutional medicine and psychiatric practice suddenly took on a different perspective and the primary needs were to mobilise services within the community.

It was almost impossible to see the situation in Charleston as not being one of extreme sadness and loss due to the fact that almost everywhere one looked, almost everywhere one went, there were people displaced, homeless, and in psychologic shock. The presence of the National Guard military units seemed to exaggerate this feeling. Suddenly, the rubble that was in the streets, the searching through the debris, the militarily-clad men in the background with bayonets and automatic weapons were not on a newsreel of another country but were present in Charleston, South Carolina. This seemed to magnify the sense of unreality.

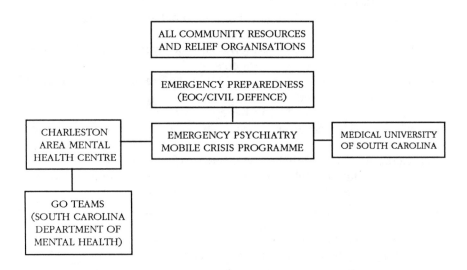

The Emergency Psychiatric Team set up a "command post" at the MHC building, which had survived the storm. Portable cellular telephones and gasoline powered generators allowed the staff to organise a central communication and treatment centre for MHC patients and walk-in emergencies.

Perhaps one of the most critical components of the disaster services was the linkage with the central office of the South Carolina Department of Mental Health (SCDMH). The department had arranged for "Go-teams" to be formed from various Department of Mental Health agencies throughout the state including community mental health centres and inpatient units. These "Go-teams" included psychiatric aides, nurses, psychologists, and people with administrative expertise. Those teams came every 3-5 days and were completely prepared to do whatever was necessary to restore the mental health of those in most need. After briefing, the "Go-teams" were quickly dispersed to various shelters around the town and were able to begin effectively dealing with peoples' mental health needs and all other needs as found appropriate.

It is important to note that in the face of disaster, one's usual job description is completely meaningless. There were few if any medications available at first, for example. Student nurses were helping co-ordinate emergency medical treatment for those in need and physicians would at times act as social workers or nurses. At first, there was little co-ordination of services. For example, we found ourselves having to deal with many of the medical problems that patients were experiencing as there was no co-ordinated effort to bring about acute medical care in the community. Over time, however, communication linkages were set up and more appropriate channels were able to be followed. One needs to be psychologically prepared and realise that in a disaster everything changes. The real suddenly becomes unreal. The familiar, totally unfamiliar. The effect is extremely disorienting and anxiety provoking. Places that were extremely familiar to people were almost unable to be recognised due to lack of lighting, signs, or other means of obtaining orientation and direction. Food, ice, batteries and generators were extremely scarce and water was undrinkable in many areas. It is important therefore for the leaders in emergency preparedness to have provisions stocked for them and their families so that they can continue to keep working at a rapid and efficient pace. Communication after Hugo was at a total standstill. We found that the use of cellular telephones in our automobiles was extremely valuable to us. However, there were times when the phones were unusable and the only way of linking up and communicating with the EOC was to make several trips per day to co-ordinate and communicate with those in the EOC. Finally, one staff member was kept present at the emergency preparedness headquarters and this allowed better communication and co-ordination. It was extremely important to centralise the communication facilities so that major needs could be made known and so that resources could be distributed in a co-ordinated and efficient way.

In addition to the "Go-teams", the SCDMH sent down teams of two SCDMH security officers per 12 hour shift. One was asked to guard our drug supplies and the other was available to accompany the mobile crisis team on calls occurring in the Charleston community. In the usual situation, our emergency team asks local law enforcement officers to join us only if necessary. However, after the hurricane, local police were relatively unavailable since they were involved in traffic control or prevention of criminal activities, such as looting. The area was placed under martial law and a curfew was imposed, making the populace very fearful and apprehensive. The armed soldiers of the National Guard began to appear everywhere.

Because of a lack of resources and the presence of overwhelming psychologic trauma, it quickly became apparent that our mobile outreach capabilities were needed throughout the community. The local emergency rooms were becoming rapidly overcrowded due to the large number of accidental injuries in the community (e.g. chainsaw accidents, cuts from broken glass or nails, fractures caused by falls, and traffic-related injuries due to the absence of electricity and traffic signals). We therefore decided to treat as many people as possible at their home or shelter. As the official civil defence co-ordinators for emergency mental health care, we were able to travel through restricted areas in an unencumbered fashion, and could also network with other systems for badly needed supplies such as food, water and medicines.

Scheduling of crisis workers was critically important. Since different members of the emergency psychiatry team returned to town at different times and since different clinicians had different stresses and different amounts of personal damages, it was important to assign clinical teams in a schedule which was made up several days at a time. Scheduling also had to be fluid given the level of exhaustion of various people and their ongoing personal needs. It was also helpful to integrate members of the "Go-teams" with the emergency psychiatry team so that all responsibility for the emergency mental health care needs of the city was not in the hands of a small core of individuals who were extremely stressed victims themselves. Actually, the "Go-team" members were extremely pleased to be involved in such an outreach endeavour.

As the emergency service responded to community calls, the most important initial interventions focused on supportive listening. Each person seen in crisis had a unique and often heroic story to tell.

Case example 1

A man with chronic schizophrenic in his early 20's was seen for exacerbation of his psychosis. He had stayed in his home during the hurricane whilst his house was destroyed around him. He appeared to be in a state of emotional shock and said he "couldn't stand the voices". We listened to him, gave him something to drink (bottled water, a precious commodity), some haloperidol and a few hugs. After two hours he felt better. Two days later our team happened to see him at the busiest shelter, where he had been volunteering to help others. He smiled and asked, "remember me?"

Traditional lines of professional practice had to be blurred at times. Primary care responsibilities often had to be dealt with before psychiatric intervention.

Case example 2

Numerous indigent people were in shelters, lacking medications for chronic medical illnesses. A psychiatry professor spent several hours on the phone in an effort to procure medical supplies. His energetic efforts allowed many chronically ill people to restart treatment with insulin, antihypertensives, and anticonvulsants.

Because of the severe shortage of beverages, many patients in alcohol withdrawal began to present for emergency evaluation.

Case example 3

A homeless woman was seen at a shelter one week after the storm. She had stayed in her beachfront home during the hurricane, clutching her dog in an upstairs closet while the wind and waves destroyed most of her beach house. The following day she went on a whisky drinking binge which lasted 3 days. Upon examination, we found her to be in alcohol withdrawal delirium, complicated by severe pancreatitis. We referred her to an internal medicine ward for emergency treatment.

In addition to seeing acute psychiatric crises within the local community, we would occasionally have to assist those people from out of town who supposedly came to Charleston to assist us.

Case example 4

A manic woman from another state came to Charleston to "do God's work and help everyone in need". Unfortunately her mania caused her to be hospitalised shortly after arrival.

Several weeks after the storm, emergency psychiatric services picked up significantly (e.g., in October 1989, 188 emergency patients were seen, compared to 143 in October 1988, a 31% increase. We believe there was an increase in suicidal callers, perhaps due to mounting stressors such as increased substance abuse, loss of jobs, frustration with insurance companies and "red tape". The community's patience began to wear thin. Post traumatic stress began to develop in many.

Case example 5

A former naval officer was washed out of his bed when the storm surge broke through his windows. For several weeks he had increasing

141

anxiety and depressive symptoms with nightmares. He called the mobile team in an intoxicated, suicidal state with a loaded revolver in his hand. The team arrived at his home, talked him into relinquishing the gun and hospitalised him.

The aforementioned vignettes illustrate some of the experiences we have encountered during the aftermath of Hurricane Hugo. There seems to have been some special strengths in the response of the mobile emergency team, and some areas which might be strengthened in the future.

The emergency psychiatric programme had a plan for dealing with Hugo and this was perhaps the most critical factor in disaster preparedness. In the wake of a natural disaster, people experience a numbness of thinking which is extremely disorienting. The high impact ratio of Hugo changed the cognitive-perceptual map of Charlestonians overnight. Because of this, it was difficult, if not almost impossible to organise systems; the existence of an emergency plan was therefore critical. After emergency mental health services were set up and co-ordinated, administrative leadership was returned to those normally in charge. Normal institutional working operations were gradually re-introduced over a period of weeks, and the emergency service gradually and naturally returned to its primary focus.

The emergency team constantly interfaced with community leaders, media, members of law enforcement, social services, and other agencies. Disaster victims were deprived of vital information, and effective networking on behalf of victims frequently resolved numerous psychiatric crises.

Although the emergency team was able to resolve most crises, little provision or time existed for proper debriefing of the emergency psychiatric clinicians themselves. For example, many clinical staff worked daily for 3 or more weeks without a day off. Normal *zeitgebers* were absent due to lack of electricity, lighting etc., and this, in part, contributed to the rapid passage of time which almost went unnoticed. Clearly, provisions for proper "time out" intervals and debriefing sessions should be included in our future disaster planning. It is extremely difficult to absorb the psychologic trauma of disaster victims when one is a victim too.

During times of disaster, numerous community organisations need to work together in order to deal with the overwhelming physical and psychological trauma that results before, during and after catastrophes. It is important to have disaster preparedness plans so that numerous community organisations can quickly organise and work co-operatively. Police, fire departments, emergency medical services, military officials, as well as county, state, and federal systems need to integrate and work in a co-ordinated fashion in order to deliver immediate service to those most in need. Emergency mental health services are important in the development of disaster planning, so that immediate mental health interventions can be provided.

Appropriate mental health leadership involving administrative support is a key element. Early visibility and early interventions are of critical importance. It is important to disseminate mental health information to the public and to provide *assertive outreach* to disaster victims. This appears to be particularly appropriate for those experiencing psychiatric emergencies. Following the Hugo disaster, psychiatrically ill people responded extremely well to very little. With a hug, a dose of psychopharmacologic medicine, some hot coffee, a few words of encouragement, some patients with severe psychiatric illnesses were able to achieve a rapid state of remission. In a way, this made us further appreciate the wonder of human resiliency.

In 1974, Kinston and Rosser noted "there is evidence that specialised psychiatric skills could be useful in all phases of a disaster. However, psychiatrists are rarely called upon and their intervention is actively resisted in the early phases by other helpers and in the late phases by the victims themselves." Our experience validated only the first part of their statement. Because of our assertive approach to psychiatric emergencies, and our previous experience in working as a mobile unit within the community, we found our services were utilised completely throughout all phases of Hurricane Hugo. It was an honour for us as mental health professionals to have been available to our community at its time of greatest need.

REFERENCES

KINSTON, W. & ROSSER, K. (1974) Disaster: Effects on Mental and Physical State *Journal of Psychosomatic Research* **19**:437-456.

Acute Applications to the Psychiatric Emergency Ward, Frederiksberg Hospital 1983 & 1988

H. Aggernæs and S. Schepelern

Introduction

As in the rest of the western world, during the past fifteen years there have been major shifts in the way in which psychiatric care has been provided in Denmark. There has been a decrease in the number of in-patients in the great mental hospitals, and an accompanying increase in district and out-patient services (Lindhardt & Reisby, 1988). As in other countries (Cooper, 1979), acute units for psychiatric emergencies in urban areas have been established - a parallel to the British A & E units for somatic emergencies.

The purpose of this paper is to describe a psychiatric emergency unit established in 1982 as an integrated part of an existing psychiatric department. Furthermore, we will describe what happened to the psychiatric service in the area. A project was designed to take account of all acute applications to the ward in 1980, 1983 and 1988.

Copenhagen is the capital of Denmark. Frederiksberg in central Copenhagen is the catchment area (85,000 inhabitants) for the general hospital situated in the centre. It has approximately 700 beds. The psychiatric department - with approximately 100 beds - was established in 1903, and was the second psychiatric department in Denmark to be integrated into a general hospital.

Prior to 1980, the department dealt only with acute in-patient psychiatry, since chronic patients were transferred to a mental hospital outside Copenhagen. In 1980 the department had established a day hospital and an out-patient clinic, but no emergency unit existed. Nevertheless, the patients arrived with their psychiatric problems. They were transferred either from the local somatic A & E unit, self-referred, or referred from a practitioner. The men waited for their psychiatric evaluation in the closed ward for men, and the women waited in the closed ward for women. It was highly unsatisfactory for patients as well as for doctors and nursing staff.

Methods

A scheme of registration was prepared. During the 12 months of 1980 the scheme was used to register almost 2500 applications (Kijne, Aggernæs, Schultz & Bjørum, 1984), but since upon statistical analysis applications were found to be independent of time of year, the periods of data collection were minimized to 2 months during the re-evaluation periods in 1983 and 1988.

The data collected were as follows:

Sex

Age

Previous psychiatric history
Living conditions
Marital status
Professional status
Way of application and status at the time of application
Acute problems presented
Acute disposition and treatment

Since the most prominent problems presented by the acute patients were connected with alcohol abuse, follow-up investigations were performed on the alcohol cohort during 9 months from 1980 and from 1983. (Aggernæs, Kijne, Schultz & Larsen, 1984; Aggernæs & Køhler, 1985a).

Results 1980

The prospective registration revealed:
1. That half of the patients had problems of alcohol addiction.
2. That one third of the patients were psychotic.
3. That half of the patients were admitted, the alcoholics mostly for 2 days.

Finally, we found that a need for psychiatric emergency assistance existed in the population, and that there was a need for a detoxification clinic as a supplement to the already existing alcohol clinic attached to the psychiatric department (Kijne et al, 1984).

The emergency unit

The emergency unit was established in 1982. The purpose was to give the population a better service - that is, immediate psychiatric help. The staff consisted of 2-3 trained nurses - depending on whether it was day, evening or night hours - an M.D. on duty who also took care of the rest of the psychiatric department, and a senior registrar on call.

The facilities were 2 sleeping rooms with 6 beds in total, 3 living rooms including the rooms for staff members, bathing facilities for patients and a little kitchen, so that the patients could get coffee, milk, a light meal etc.

The patients who stayed overnight at the emergency unit were not registered as in-patients; only a short emergency journal was filled in. This point is very important for most Danish psychiatric patients, since all psychiatric admissions in Denmark are registered in a nationwide central demographic register in Aarhus.

The observation time was limited to 24 hours, so that the patients could only stay for 1 night. There was an acute evaluation by an M.D. and a morning conference where all the patients were discussed by a senior registrar, a psychologist, a social worker and nurses from the out-patient service and the alcohol clinic. The patients who stayed overnight were re-evaluated by the senior registrar.

Results 1983

Comparison of the data from 1980 with the data from 1983 showed that the establishment of an emergency unit doubled the number of applications from 6 per day in 1980 to 12 per day in 1983. Furthermore, the catchment area in 1983 was only 60% of the original catchment area.

Not all of the applications in 1983 were acute, since a lot of patients came only to talk with the nurses, or they came on semi-acute visits to finish detoxification treatment after alcohol abuse. When corrected for change of catchment area, acute applications were 3 per day in 1980, whereas in 1985 there were 7 per day. During both years there was equal distribution of men and women among the clients. The most prominent problems during both years were alcoholism and psychosis. The number of admissions decreased from 1980 to 1983. In 1980, three-quarters of the psychotics were admitted, and almost half of the alcoholics. In 1983, the alcoholics were no longer admitted into the closed ward for 2-3 days for detoxification treatment. Rather, they stayed overnight in the emergency ward. In the case of 18% of the applications, the M.D.'s decision was an overnight stay at the unit for further evaluation the following day or for detoxification treatment.

The decrease in admissions was paralleled by an increase in out-patient service. In 1980, only 7% of the patients were recommended out-patient service, whereas in 1983 18% of the patients were treated acutely as out-patients, either by crisis therapy in the emergency unit or by one of the psychologists or psychiatrists on the ward (Aggernæs & Køhler, 1985b).

Reasons for 800 overnight stays 1983

Alcoholism accounted for 64% of the overnight stays. It seems as if the emergency unit fulfilled the need for a detoxification clinic, since follow-up investigations of the alcoholics showed better outcome in 1983 than in 1980.

Psychosis amounted to 12%, suicidal behaviour 15%, and other reasons 9%. Actually, from 1980 to 1983 a decline in applications made because of suicidal behaviour was registered. The majority of alcoholics had an overnight stay instead of being hospitalised; in 1983 only 15% of the alcoholics were admitted, most of these because of very bad social conditions or delirium.

Conclusion of investigation 1983

1. There was a 20% decrease in acute admissions, but only a slight decrease in the number of beds used, since the decreased admissions were the 2-day admissions of the alcoholics, whilst the psychotic - and schizophrenic patients especially - were admitted as before, yet stayed longer on the ward (1 to 2 months) since they were no longer transferred to mental hospitals outside Copenhagen.
2. The alcoholics were treated without admission. The follow-up investigations from the alcohol cohort in 1980 and 1983 showed that

the results in 1983 were equal or even better after 9 months; that is, that the treatment outcome for an alcoholic was independent of acute admission compared to acute overnight stay.

3. Establishing an emergency unit increased acute out-patient service, and further - perhaps not surprisingly - allowed the appearance of a huge number of non-acute applications at the unit, up to 40% in total. These patients did not talk with an M.D., and were thus not registered on the scheme (Aggernæs & Køhler, 1985b).

1983 - 1988

From 1983 to 1987 a 30% increase of applications was registered. We therefore wanted to repeat the investigation in order to try to explain this increase.

Was it the non-acute applications which increased?

Had the unit's function changed?

In the meantime - that is, from 1981 - all of Copenhagen had been sectorised, thus the psychiatric department at Frederiksberg Hospital now takes care of all psychiatric cases in the catchment area, acute as well as chronic. No patients are sent to mental hospitals outside of Copenhagen, but district and out-patient services have increased. During the 1980's the number of out-patient consultations has increased to 16,000 per year.

Results 1988

The registration period was 2 months. The number of patients who applied was 369, presenting in total 874 times. 66% presented only once; the remainder attended a median of 3 times, with variations from 2 to 70. (The latter was a young man in need of a social institution, for whom the department of social security could not find a suitable place. We did not feel it appropriate to admit him, because his problems were of a social and not a psychiatric nature. Despite our resistance, 1 month later he was admitted, but that is the way it is - we still lack adequate accommodation when the patients' problems are merely social. Social institutions are essential, if the number of psychiatric beds are to diminish.)

The applications can be divided into two groups: 379 acute and 495 non-acute applications, all of which were registered on the scheme.

Compared to 1983, the number of acute applications from women had increased, but the corresponding number from men had decreased, so that the total number of acute applications had stabilised. The number of non-acute applications increased, 63% compared to 40% in 1983.

The age distribution remained much the same. The majority of both sexes were between 30 and 39 years, and as in earlier years most of the patients had formerly been treated at a psychiatric department before application. In 1980 half of the patients were referred by their general practitioner. In 1983 this number had decreased to 1/4 of the applications, and in 1988 only 1/10 of the patients were referred to the unit by G.P.'s., the rest being self-referred. Table 1 on the following page shows the reasons for acute applications. Compared to 1983 a significant increase in women with alcohol addiction problems was observed, and a slight (insignificant) decrease in drug addiction. The number and percentage of psychoses were equal for men and women and unchanged from 1983. The number of neurotic conditions was unchanged from 1983. There was an even further decrease in the number of women with suicidal behaviour. This change was also observed from 1980 to 1983. Maybe the establishment of the unit had created a possibility for the women to turn up before behaving suicidally, or maybe the women behaved like the men, since it seems as if women have adapted men's reaction pattern to alcohol habits. There was a significant increase in men applying acutely with no exact psychiatric problems, rather loneliness and/or poor social status. Most of these men were chronic schizophrenics and/or had problems of addiction.

TABLE 1
Reasons for acute applications 1988

	Women %	Men %
Alcoholism	56*	45
Drug Addiction/Narcomania	9	6
Psychosis	34	34
Neurosis etc.	12	11
Reactio Affectiva (T.S.)	9*	7
Loneliness/Bad social status	15	24*
Other	18	17

* $p < 0.05$ compared to 1983

Table 2 on the next page shows the reasons for non-acute applications. The most frequent reason amongst women was alcoholism, and psychosis amongst men. 19 of the 20 registered non-acute applications from drug addicts were from 4 schizophrenic men already treated in the department as out-patients. 10 or 15 years ago these patients would have been chronic in-patients of a mental hospital. Now we try to integrate them into the community, but - as with these 4 - with little success, since they had nowhere to go, and no one would accept them other than the psychiatric ward and staff.

TABLE 2
Reasons for non-acute applications 1988

	Women %	Men %
Alcoholism	45	28
Drug Addiction/Narcomania	0	6
Psychosis	32	37
Neurosis etc.	4	4
Reactio Affectiva (T.S.)	2	1
Loneliness/Bad social status	6	9
Other	11	15

Table 3 shows marital status. The reason for the quotation marks is the fact that it is very common in Denmark - especially in urban areas - for couples to live together without getting formally married. Thus we did not register the patients as "married or unmarried", but as "living alone or as a couple". As you can see, a greater number of the men lived alone or were homeless compared to the women. The data concerning the men were unchanged from 1983 to 1988. The figures for the women had changed since 1983 when 53% of the women lived alone. This probably reflects the fact that a greater number of female alcoholics come to the unit than before, and compared to the schizophrenic patients these women have less psychopathology, and are therefore more likely to live in a family.

TABLE 3
"Marital Status" registered in acute applications 1988

	Women %	Men %
Living Alone	41*	63
As a couple	45*	20
With others	14	14
No home		3

* p <0.05 compared to 1983)

150

Table 4 shows that less than 1/4 of the patients were working, 20% of the women and 27% of the men. Almost half of the applications were patients living on disability pensions. Compared to 1983 the number of patients with pensions had increased, and unemployment and sick leave had decreased, perhaps because of the revision of the pension law in 1984. It is now possible in Denmark to get a pension on account of social conditions and not only on account of chronic illness.

TABLE 4

Professional activity registered in acute applications 1988

	Women %	Men %
At work	20	27
Unemployed	9*	20
Sick Leave > 5 weeks	9	4*
Disability Pension	49	43
Education	5	
Other	8	6

* p <0.05 compared to 1983

Table 5 (on the next page) shows the dispositions taken. Only 1/4 of the acutely applying patients were admitted. Compared to 1983 this was a significant decrease for women applicants. Regarding both sexes, there was an increase of out-patient treatment, which included already established treatment regimes and acute crisis therapy. Very few were referred to treatment by a G.P., probably reflecting that different sections of the population seek help in different places. (You may see the same pattern when it comes to the population's seeking help against alcoholism. The sections who apply to the alcohol clinics do not apply at the emergency unit.) There was a decrease in men transferred to alcohol clinics. 26% of women and 28% of men left the ward without appointment, either because their problems were solved, or because they left before treatment was finished. In 16% of the acute applied cases it was estimated that the patients had not had optimal treatment (Schepelern, Kjærager, Musenfryd & Aggernæs, 1990).

TABLE 5
Dispositions after acute applications 1988

	Women %	Men %
Acute Admission	24*	23
Acute/Continued Out-patient Treatment	33*	28*
General Practitioner/ Specialist	6	4
Alcohol Clinic	4	6*
No appointment	26	28
Other	7	11

* p <0.05 compared to 1983

Conclusion

Establishment of an emergency unit:
1. Decreases the number of acute admissions;
2. Increases out-patient treatment;
3. Makes it possible to treat alcoholics without psychiatric admission;
4. Decreases female suicidal behaviour, and
5. Functions as a contact place for the chronic schizophrenic patients in the catchment area - patients who have nowhere else to go.

REFERENCES

AGGERNÆS, K.H.; KIJNE, B.; SCHULTZ, V. & LARSEN, J.K. (1984) Applications to a Psychiatric Admission Department on Account of Conditions Connected with Alcohol *Ugeskr Læger* **146**:538-542.

AGGERNÆS, K.H. & KØHLER, D. (1985a) Acute Treatment of Patients with Alcohol Problems in the Psychiatric Emergency Unit at Frederiksberg Hospital *Ugeskr Læger* **147**:3341-3343.

AGGERNÆS, K.H. & KØHLER, D. (1985b) Applications to the Psychiatric Admission Department at Frederiksberg Hospital after Establishment of an Emergency Unit *Ugeskr Læger* **147**:3273-3276.

COOPER, J.E. (1979) *Crisis Admission Units and Emergency Psychiatric Services* København: WHO Regional Office for Europe.

KIJNE, B.; AGGERNÆS, H.; SCHULTZ, V. & BJØRUM, N. (1984) Emergency Applications to a Psychiatric Admission Department *Ugeskr Læger* **146**:449-453.

LINDHARDT, A. & REISBY, N. (1988) Development of Hospital-Based District Psychiatry in Denmark: Status from 1982 to 1987 *Ugeskr Læger* **150**:14-18.

SCHEPELERN, E.S.; KJÆRAGER, W.; MUSENFRYD, P. & AGGERNÆS, K.H. (1990) Alteration in the Function of a Psychiatric Admission Department *Ugeskr Læger* **152**:1075-1077.

Establishing a New Crisis Service in Western Australia
Michael Ash

This paper reflects on the professional and political challenges associated with and involved in setting up a Psychiatric Emergency Service.

Background

The service is the first of its kind in the state of Western Australia. The state is the largest single state in the world, approximately twelve times the size of the United Kingdom, yet with a population of only 1.5 million people of a wide multicultural background.

The majority of the people (1 million) live in the capital city of Perth, located in the south western part of the state. The rest are distributed throughout the state which has three other relatively small cities, and scattered small towns.

To put this in perspective: it would take 5 days hard driving for a colleague in the far north to reach another in the south of the state. Much of the inland area is hostile and uninhabited desert.

Many of the large farms and cattle stations are hundreds of thousands of acres in size and hundreds of miles from any regular health services. They are of course served by the famous Australian Royal Flying Doctor Service, but this service is not a psychiatric service and remote towns are serviced by a visiting psychiatrist possibly once a month. Even so, to see the psychiatrist may take a 5-10 hour journey.

Catchment area

Fortunately the majority of people live in the Perth metropolitan area, itself geographically bigger than greater London. The Psychiatric Emergency Team therefore effectively has a catchment area size of 160km by 50km. The largest portion of its workload is within the central metropolitan area, 40km by 20km.

The only secure psychiatric beds are in the city of Perth. People suffering from a relatively minor psychiatric disorder that can be treated on a voluntary basis are therefore admitted to a general medical bed in a Regional Hospital.

People who are compulsorily admitted because they are either disturbed or lacking in insight and unwilling to be treated are therefore flown to Perth and admitted to Graylands Hospital, the larger of the two psychiatric hospitals in Perth.

Composition of the team

The team comprises of a Nurse-Co-ordinator (who is essentially the team manager), plus seven additional Psychiatric Community Nurses with a wide background of clinical experience; a full time Psychiatrist (the Clinical Director), a clerk/typist and four additional psychiatrists who provide, along with the Clinical Director, an on-call after-hours service.

Duty hours

The team is actually on duty from 8am until 11pm with an on-call roster after this time. Beyond 11pm, 'phones are diverted to the major psychiatric hospital and calls are received by the nursing supervisor who triages the calls and then pages the "on-call" nurse from the team. The PET nurse may then contact the caller and if unable to resolve the problem over the phone will undertake a home visit to make an assessment. At this stage the duty Psychiatrist will be called by the nurse if required, or the nurse may assess first and then decide if medical support/intervention is required.

Of all calls received, 35% result in a home visit and of these between 25-50% will also be seen by the Psychiatrist.

The reason for the team

The Western Australian Council for Social Services (WACOSS), an umbrella organisation for over 400 non-government agencies concerned with a wide range of social services, ranging from accommodation, welfare, refuges, homeless day centres and many self-help groups, was the major lobbyist in demanding after-hours mobile emergency service.

The people and various groups that they represent had experienced great difficulty with residents or clients who exhibited a wide range of psychological/psychiatric symptoms and for whom they could obtain no help.

The police were powerless unless an offence had been committed. Accident and Emergency departments often gave a low priority to the "Psychiatric Patient" if indeed the person was willing to attend an emergency department.

PART ONE

"So you want to commit professional suicide".

As our beginings fortuitously conincided with an election year, funding was available in order to "do something". Everyone had their own idea as to what that "something" should be and of course, as is the nature of psychiatry throughout the world, their "something" was bigger and better than the next person's "something".

So politically speaking: "If I can't have the money nor can you and anyway you should do it my way, your way won't work"!

We did the rounds of the agencies, seeking to determine what they wanted from the service prior to its commencement and then went to our fellow professionals to explain these needs.

We were invited to a major teaching hospital to discuss our service and were asked "what's all this about an emergency service? We already provide an emergency service to the city". Unfortunately, insightless, psychotic patients in crisis could not make use of general hospital emergency departments in which they had to sit in a waiting room for hours before receiving attention.

Nevertheless we were told that our ideas could not, should not and would not work. We were "committing professional suicide" and would be "unemployable in six months". The nurses would assess patients who would then suicide; we would all consequently be sued, and unable ever to raise our psychiatric heads again.

We all realised such comments were intended as expressions of concern on our behalf and had nothing to do with the setting up of a new and anxiety-provoking service which by its very nature would be likely to take a high public profile!

Our project needed the support of the Nursing Unions to agree to an alteration of the normal working hours of the community nurses. This raised the issue that it would thus create a precedent and feelings - particularly by those people who normally worked 9-5 - that maybe it should not be allowed.

There was only enough money to have a team of nurses, so many allied health workers thought that change should not happen until a fully multidisciplinary team could be established.

We were totally overwhelmed by the lack of support from many of our health professional colleagues, the very people from whom we had naively expected the greatest support. However, we were reassured by the amount of verbal support we were receiving from the agencies for whom we were likely to provide a service.

The budget allocation for the year was $300,000 (approximately 150,000 pounds sterling), for everything - including equipment, staffing and all running costs.

The premises were conveniently located in the inner city area but were basically unsuitable for an operations base, having major car parking problems.

None of the staff had any direct experience in working with a crisis service. Further, the team was together for only six days before becoming operational, during which time we had to obtain disused furniture from vacated government offices and transport it ourselves; set up the office; decide on running and operational protocols; create rosters; and, very importantly, try to form a team.

Many of our requests for simple additional items were subject to obstructive questions in order to delay or deny their procurement. Others thought they knew what we wanted or should have.

We began to rely very heavily on the concept that "in crisis there are many opportunities" and of course we knew an election was to be held very soon!

We were indeed about to commit professional suicide, but we had a few things going for us: namely, a huge unfilled need for such a service and thus a major political lobby group on our behalf if we could deliver a satisfactory service.

We had a hand-picked team of mature, experienced and talented nurses, who had a wide range of skills and above all could work independently. They had, between them, worked in the majority of the psychiatric services (both public and private) in the city and had a huge range of local knowledge and each enjoyed the clinical confidence of their fellow workers.

The rest of the team comprised of: a newly qualified psychiatrist who was popular because of his charm, sense of humour and dedication to duty; a clerk typist who was formerly the secretary to the Director of Community Psychiatric Nursing; the Team Co-ordinator, who, although resident in Australia for only 18 months, was one of the most experienced nurse managers in the state, having held various senior nursing management positions in the UK. The interpersonal and political skills of the Team Co-ordinator were to be used extensively.

PART TWO
"Resuscitation of the professionally dead".

Our beginnings were more of a wishful idea than a reality, but we realised that if we waited until everything was in place and properly formulated you would not be reading this now!

It is said that "In crisis there are many opportunities"; we decided that in crisis there is also the basis for a corporate plan and corporate identity. How, therefore, to turn this good idea, this vision of the inner city agencies, into reality?

We had to create a product that had identity, that was marketable and above all else that was going to provide the services that the customers wanted, "customers" here being the consumers of mental health services and their relatives and carers.

We needed a name that could realistically describe our function, did not conflict with the Western Australian Department of Community Services "Crisis Care" team of Social Workers, and was not too lengthy. The name we settled for ("The Psychiatric Emergency Team") came from one of our Regional Nursing co-ordinators; abbreviated to "PET", it is short, snappy and easily remembered. Importantly, this helps to give our service a marketable identity.

We designed our own letterheads and produced a simple, pocket-sized folder describing our activities. All staff had their own business cards, and again this was to help promote a feeling of identity within the team and was part of the professional image-building process.

Having a limited budget, it seemed we must either provide a limited, prioritised service with a very narrowly defined selection criteria, or give a broadly-based but ineffective service which would fulfil a role only superficially.

We decided to do neither; instead, we returned to crisis theory to redefine the problem and then, more importantly, the ownership of these problems. The first problem was to give good service; we knew we had the skill to do this and were therefore happy to "own" this problem. The second problem was the cost of being effective; this, we decided, was a problem for the Health Department to "own". We were providing a good service.

We decided to develop the service in several ways:

1. As a direct service, providing assessment and treatment to the client in their own environment. This could be in the patients' own home or in a social services agency or indeed in the police station. We always visit the client and are only accessed via the telephone.
2. As a source of information about any relevant services pertaining to the mentally ill and, importantly, how to successfully access them.
3. As a referral agency, making direct referrals to other services on behalf of clients, such services including clinics, hospitals and individual therapists both in the public and private sectors.
4. As a community education facility, ever ready to talk on any aspect of the care or management of the mentally ill. To run workshops or seminars, give professional advice to the many self-help organisations. To produce mental health/illness literature, including drug information booklets, phrased in simple language for the patient and family, and to give guidelines on how best to get the most from the health care system.
5. To collect data on all aspects of our activities, in order to justify our existence and to use as the basis for any future planning. Simply, if you don't count, you don't count.
6. To be ambassadors for community nursing and psychiatric services in general. To do this we must be politically aware; not along party lines but rather in regard to the dynamics of a large bureaucracy, and the posturing and manipulative manoeuvring that occurs. When dealing with difficult problems or attracting good publicity we try to ensure that everybody comes out feeling OK, with their egos intact. We go for a "WIN-WIN" situation!
7. To take an active role in supporting the self-help agencies and use them and the various functions and study days as opportunities to promote the team.

With regard to this last point, we are, for example, actively involved in the annual National Mental Health Week and were responsible for facilitating a very striking publicity poster. That may seem minor but very importantly we used the art therapy department of the local psychiatric hospital to provide us with artwork which, with the help of the Health

Promotion Department of the Authority, we turned into a very striking poster. We then had the poster mounted and presented by the Minister for Health to the patients who had done the original artwork at the opening ceremony of Mental Health Week.

This was a major media event which all the TV channels attended. It was good publicity for all involved and we were of course seen as the instigators of the scheme, and thus generated a great deal of support.

We learnt to use manipulation and regardless of the bad press such a tactic has attracted in the past, it is a sophisticated management tool which should be turned into an art form. We did.

PART THREE
"Resurrection"

When you do a good job you feel good and can tell yourself you did well.

When you really do a very good job other people tell you "Hey, you did well there". But when you do a very, very good job other people tell everyone else "You know, those people from the PET are something special". They begin to lobby on your behalf.

When you reach this stage you know have succeeded, but it is not enough just to let this happen; there will always be a few cynical diehards who want to create unsolicited, adverse criticism on your behalf, so you must create your own good publicity and generate a stream of commendations to your political masters.

You must ensure that the various professional bodies now welcome you into the fold and begin to lobby on your behalf. This essentially happens when you do them a favour - usually with a particularly difficult client. (The one that is dumped into the "too difficult to manage" basket like a red hot coal and promptly referred on.)

All the various mental health self-help agencies began to co-ordinate their support and lobbying to the Minister of Health on our behalf.

The Royal Australian and New Zealand College of Psychiatrists made a formal submission to the Department supporting our need for continued funding.

Our Clinical Director has been invited to address a National Conference of the RANZCP and talk about the team.

Success feeds on success. The Psychiatric Emergency Team was set up as a political initiative. By providing an excellent level of professional, caring service, we have become, so Ministers say, the most effective and successful Health Department initiative in recent years.

Our financial problems will no doubt continue but we will survive.

We have arrived, we are here to stay!

160

Training of Crisis Intervention Team Members

Helen Cleak

Introduction

My task as a lecturer at La Trobe University is to prepare students for their social work professional roles. As a practitioner working in the Emergency Department of an acute hospital I am aware of the field's criticism of the schools of social work for their emphasis on concepts, theories and constructs and a detachment from the day to day demands of practice.

Thus, the first aim in the development of a course to teach crisis intervention to final year social work students has been to be mindful of the responsibility of trying to bridge the gap between education and practice.

Educators must attempt to justify their conception of therapeutic change as well as the aims and goals of their training programmes. If the goals and behaviours are clearly defined and the teaching methods appropriately chosen and implemented, then the programme should be more effective.

The second major aim, then, is to clearly articulate the objectives and goals that need to be achieved by the end of the teaching period. Evaluation becomes an important component of the course and trainees must be able to demonstrate specific competencies and acquisition of skills otherwise we have no guarantee that real learning has occurred.

In defining objectives, I have had to decide on the major philosophical educational direction of the course content. I have chosen a generic approach which focuses on crises as stemming from a particular kind of hazardous event rather than on the psychodynamics and unique ecological matrix of the individual in crisis.

In brief, the generic approach emphasises the specific situational and maturational events occurring to a significant population group, and intervention is oriented to the crisis related to those specific events. However, I emphasise the uniqueness of the individual cases and the fact that finer discrimination is needed to account for these individual differences.

My third aim, therefore, is to engender in the student the need to look at the psychological dynamics of each individual in crisis, which is usually achieved through the experiential part of the course.

With these three riders in place, I would like to turn to an examination of the crisis intervention course in more detail. (See also Appendix I.)

I have tried to develop a didactic - experiential programme. In crisis intervention, the student must obtain a preliminary knowledge of the theoretical underpinnings to the skills being taught.

Content of the course
(see also Appendix II)

1. Firstly we must agree on a *definition* of a crisis: A change in a person's circumstances which leads to disruptive feelings which can interfere with their learning to deal with change.

   People in crisis are passing through a phase of disturbed psychological equilibrium on the way to a new equilibrium. People in crisis suddenly face different circumstances which demand different coping responses from them. The crisis, therefore, is a time of cognitive disorganisation and emotional disturbances and also a time of increased vulnerability to external influences.

2. Practitioners must be able to recognise a crisis in time to work with it, before maladjustments have set in and change-producing anxiety has receded, e.g. Stages of a Crisis.

3. The Eriksonian developmental model explicates the biopsychosocial maturational stages of man, the inherent potential for crisis, and the relevant tasks required for subsequent maturation. Crisis-handling is the basis for continued growth of competence.

4. The generic approach looks at a variety of situational crises and the elements within these that need to be addressed e.g. divorce, death, mastectomy, hospitalisation, disasters.

5. Emphasises the systematic approach. The major task is to clear the paths for recovery; to make sure that the process is going forward and to make resources available as needed in each case.

   The immediate goal of crisis intervention is helping people to recognise and work through their emotional responses of shock, anxiety, anger and depression which are known to occur during crises. The longer-term goal is restructuring coping patterns and so produce growth.

6. The experiential aspect has great value in the teaching of any therapeutic activity for often trainees struggle for too long with abstract concepts, before they see them as having any relevance to their clinical experience.

My approach is to take the theory out of the classroom setting and into actual interview situations, so that students can practice sound diagnostic and interactive competencies.

Without "live" subjects course members role play for each other which, apart from giving them interview practice, allows them to experience being on the receiving end of good and bad skills performance.

The essence of this approach is that the trainee is provided with intensive practice and the learning process is reinforced with the use of feedback, particularly on video tape.

Three major areas of skill acquisition are required to be demonstrated by the trainee.

1. *Structuring Skills*: The trainees must be generally active and provide some structuring early on. These skills include directiveness, information-gathering, clarity etc.
2. *Relationship Skills*: The trainees must have the basic ability to establish a positive relationship, e.g. use of empathy, warmth, genuineness.
3. *Conceptual Skills*: The trainee must be able to integrate the crisis intervention framework for the individual situation.

Burnout

The danger inherent in crisis intervention work is personal burnout, which results in lowered morale, substandard work and attrition.

All helping professionals experience the first stages of burnout as they move from training to the real difficulties and limitations of their profession and specific work environments.

There are a number of reasons why crisis intervention workers are prone to burnout:

1. As in other areas of counselling, assessing the degree of therapeutic success is often difficult to accomplish. Evaluating whether one is doing a good job and whether your client is benefiting from the intervention is essential but complex.
2. Doing something positive for your client is one of the strongest goals that crisis intervention workers bring to their work and the lack of feedback that often occurs is very frustrating.
3. External stressors that impinge on crisis workers include multiple cases that are usually complex and require urgent attention. She/he is often required to work on her/his own; unable to finish work until the case is completed or able to be left for the next worker; and often experiences inadequate leadership and opportunity for support debriefing.

The course should emphasize the tendency for crisis intervention workers to suffer from burnout, especially amongst women where it occurs four times more frequently. There should be discussion about strategies, both personal and organisationally to protect themselves against burnout. These include:

1. The need to structure free time and to set up boundaries between work and home - this can sometimes be difficult for residential workers and those "on" on "on-call" systems.
2. The right to demand adequate supervision to allow time for ventilation, support and on-going skills development.

3. Setting realistic and achievable goals. The helping professions have been identified as a group who have high expectations of themselves and are therefore easily discouraged and frustrated when goals are not met.
4. Variety in work-related tasks is often a useful strategy so that they are not always working in high-stress situations.
5. Encouraging them to input to decision-making in areas that affect their work life. This can help to reduce their sense of powerlessness.

REFERENCES

AGIULERA, D. & MESSICK, J. (1986) *Crisis Intervention: Theory and Methodology* Missouri: C.V. Mosby Company.

BOYCE, L. & SCOTT, V. (1986) Curriculum Planning for Social Work in Health Care: The Practitioner's View *Australian Social Work* **39**:37-43.

EGAN, G. (1975) *The Skilled Helper* California: Brooks/Cole Publishing Co.

GILLILAND, B. & JONES, R. (1988) *Crisis Intervention Strategies* California: Brooks/Cole Publishing Co.

GOLAN, N. (1978) *Treatment in Crisis Situations* New York: The Free Press.

HOFFMAN, D. & REMMEL (1975) Uncovering the Precipitant in Crisis Intervention *Social Casework* **56**:259-268

IVEY, A. & AUTHIER, J. (1978) *Microcounselling* Springfield, Illinois: Charles C. Thomas.

LUKTON, R. (1982) Myths and Realities of Crisis Intervention *Social Casework* **63**:276-286.

LANE, H. (1982) Towards the Preparation of Social Work Specialists in Health Care *Social Casework* **7**:230-234

RATCLIFF, N. (1988) Stress and Burnout in the Helping Profession *Social Casework* **61**:147-154.

ROSENBERG, B. (1975) Planned Short-Term Treatment in Developmental Crises *Social Casework* **56**:195-204.

SNOOK, V. (1984) Burnout and Whose Responsibility *Australian Social Work* **37**:19-23.

SOSKIS, C. (1985) *Social Work in the Emergency Room* New York: Springer Publishing Company.

STREET, E. & TREACHER, A. (1980) Microtraining and Family Therapy Skills - Towards a Possible Synthesis *Journal of Family Therapy* **2**:243-257.

TRUAX, C. & CARKHUFF, R. (1967) *Towards Effective Counselling and Psychotherapy* Chicago: Aldine.

TURNER, F. (ed.) (1979) *Social Work Treatment* New York: The Free Press.

APPENDIX I

Social Work theory and practice Life crises

Course description

The purpose of this subject is to introduce students to the theoretical concepts of crises that people encounter as they move through the life cycle. A range of developmental and situational crises will be explored as well as possible intervention strategies.

Course objectives

The objectives of the course are that the student shall:

1. Develop an understanding of the evaluation and development of crisis intervention theory and its basic concepts.
2. Appreciate the universality of crisis situations as "normal" and inevitable in human growth and development.
3. Look at types of crises that people can face, including maturational and situational crises.
4. Become familiar with these concepts, through the use of a variety of case examples drawn from the health and welfare field including working with the bereaved, dying children, survivors of natural disasters, etc.
5. Develop an understanding of the preventive implication of timing and focussed interventions during stress.
6. Learn the principles and techniques of working with individuals and families in crisis and time-limited situations.

Method of instruction

This elective will be taught via lecture and discussion methods, along with the use of case material, video tapes and student participation and presentation.

Students will be expected to complete weekly reading and be prepared to discuss them in class.

Essential texts:

(One of these two books should be used as a basic text.)

- Aguilera, D. & Messick, J. (1986) *Crisis Intervention: Theory and Methodology* Missouri: C.V. Mosby Company.

- Gilliland, B.& Jones, R. (1988) *Crisis Intervention Strategies* California: Brooks/Cole.

APPENDIX II

Social Work theory and practice Life crises

Week 1
- Introduction to the course
- Evolution & development of crisis theory
- Definition of a crisis
- Elements in the crisis situation
- Reactions to the state of active crisis

Readings   Golan, N. (1978) *Treatment in Crisis Situations*
New York: The Free Press

Lindemann, N.E. (1974) Symptomatology and Management of Acute Grief. In H. Parad. (ed) *Crisis Intervention: Selected Readings* New York: F.S.A.A.

Rapoport, L. (1974) The State of Crisis: Some Theoretical Considerations. In H. Parad (op.cit.)

Aguilera, D. & Messick, J. (op.cit.) Ch. 1.

Gilliland, B. & Jones, R. (op.cit.) Ch. 1.

Week 2
- Types of crisis situations
- Maturational and developmental crises

Readings   Erikson, E. (1963) *Childhood and Society* New York: W.W. Norton. Chapter 7 Eight Ages of Man

Golan, N. (op.cit.) Chapter 8.

Rosenberg, B. (1975) Planned Short-Term Treatment in Developmental Crises *Social Casework* **56**:195-241.

Aguilera, D. & Messick, J. (op.cit.) Ch. 7.

Scherz, F. (1971) Maturational Crises and Child Interaction. *Social Casework* **52**:362-369.

Week 3
- Transitional crises e.g. Divorce
- Situational crises   e.g. Ageing

Readings   Golan, N. (op.cit.) Chapter 9.

Wiseman, R. (1975) Crisis Theory and the Process of Divorce *Social Casework* **56**:205-212.

Counts, R. & Sacks, A. (1985) The Need for Crisis Intervention During Marital Separation *Social Work* **30**:146-150.

Aguilera, D. & Messick, J. (op.cit.) Ch. 6

Freeman, E. (1984) Multiple Losses in the Elderly: An Ecological Approach *Social Casework* **65**:287-296.

Week 4
- Situational crises   e.g. Death
- A typical grief reaction
- Disaster situations

Readings   Stringham, J.; Riley, J. & Ross, A. (1982) Silent Birth: Mourning a Stillborn Baby *Social Work* **63**:322-327.

Goldberg, S. (1973) Family Task and Reactions in the Crisis of Death *Social Casework* **54**:398-405.

Kellehear (1984) The Sociology of Death and Dying *Australian Social Work* **37**.

Beneoek, E. (1985) Children and Disaster: Emergency Issues. *Psychiatric Referrals* **15**:168-172.

Jones, I. & Jones, A. (1988) Psychological Consequences of Armed Hold Up *Australian Family Physician* **17**:447-450

Gilliland, B. & Jones, R. *Crisis Intervention Strategies* Chs. 3,7,10,11 and 12 (op.cit.)

Dufka, C. (1988) The Mexico City Earthquake Disaster. *Social Casework* **60**:162-170.

Week 5   • Suicidal behaviour

Readings   Klugman, D.; Litman, R. & Wold, C. (1965) Suicide: Answering the Cry for Help *Social Work* **10**:43-49.

Fujimura, L.; Weis, D. & Cochran, J. (1985) Suicide: Dynamics and Implications for Counselling *Journal of Counselling and Development* **63**:612-615.

Hepworth, D.; Farley, O. & Griffiths, J. (1988) Clinical Work with Suicidal Adolescents and their Families *Social Casework* **69**:195-203.

Week 6   • When to use crisis intervention
               • Short-Term casework - theoretical perspectives
               • Stages of crisis resolution

Readings   Golan, N. (1969) When is a Client in Crisis? *Social Casework* **50**:389-394.

Hoffman, D. & Remmel, M. (1975) Uncovering the Precipitant in Crisis Intervention *Social Casework* **56**:259-267.

Aguilera, D. & Messick, J. (op.cit.) Ch. 5.

Lukton, R. (1982) Myths and Realities of Crisis Intervention *Social Casework* **63**:276-285.

Gilliland, B. & Jones, R. (op.cit.) Ch. 2.

Week 7   • Social Work strategies and techniques in crisis resolution

Readings   Golan, N. (op.cit.) Ch. 6.

Cormican, E. (1977) Task Centred Model for Work with the Aged *Social Casework* **58**:490-494.

Zaro, J.S. (1977) *A Guide for Beginning Psychotherapists* Cambridge: Cambridge University Press Ch.10.

Reid, W. (1979) Task Centred Treatment. In F. Turner (ed.) *Social Work Treatment* 479-495 New York: The Free Press.

Week 8   In-class examination (1 hour)

Week 9   Review